MYSTERY IN
NEWFOUNDLAND

Frances Shelley Wees

Mystery in
Newfoundland

ILLUSTRATED BY DOUGLAS BISSET

ABELARD-SCHUMAN
London New York Toronto

London	*New York*	*Toronto*
Abelard-Schuman	Abelard-Schuman	Abelard-Schuman
Limited	Limited	Canada Limited
8 King St. WC2	6 West 57th St.	896 Queen St. W.

Printed in the United States of America

"For Mark, who well knows why."

MYSTERY IN
NEWFOUNDLAND

ALASKA

Atlantic Ocean

CANADA

NEWFOUNDLAND

UNITED
STATES

Avalon

St. Johns

Father Duffy's Well

ATLANTIC
OCEAN

Crewes' Pond

Charity's
Garden

Cave

St. Mary's Bay

CHAPTER

1

THE PATTERSONS were in Newfoundland. They were living in the Newfoundland Hotel, in St. John's.

Big Ben Patterson had left his family there while he made a geological trip to Labrador. The children had never lived in a hotel before. Hotels were full of exciting strangers, coming and going, each one mysterious.

A stranger in this hotel could be anybody — a very rich man, coming to invest money in one of Newfoundland's just-beginning developments; a dangerous criminal coming far from the mainland to hide from the police — anybody.

Mat Patterson, eleven, was always thinking and talking about the strangers in the hotel lobby and the elevators and the restaurant, making up stories about them. Mat had a strong imagination and he read too many books; Tim and Meg were always trying to hold him down to earth.

He was reading a book now. He and Tim, twelve, were waiting in the living room of their suite for their mother and Meg, who were dressing the quicksilver twins, Peter and Patsy, so that they could all go down to breakfast. Tim was at the window, looking out through the sunshiny misty morning to the Narrows, the sea opening of St. John's Harbour, and at Cabot Tower, standing like a watchful guard on the top of Signal Hill. They had been in St. John's for five days, but this old, old city, the oldest city in North America, was still strange and new. All Newfoundland was strange and new; its ways of living, even its ways of talking. There was a lot to know about Newfoundland, more than any stranger might think.

Mat said suddenly, "I think it might have been fun to be a pirate. Dangerous, though. But all that treasure . . . crowns thick with great big rubies, and solid-gold crosses two feet high set with emeralds, and rose nobles, and pieces of eight . . . shiploads of treasure. They don't have stuff like that any more."

Tim turned from the window. Mat didn't look much like a possible pirate, sitting in a big chair with his feet curled under him, holding a stack of brightly covered books he had found at the Tourist Bureau yesterday. He wasn't big for his age. He was a first-rate baseball player and a whiz at hockey because he was fast. But he had small bones and a mop of yellow hair that always needed to be cut, and right now he had braces on his teeth so that he lisped a little. No, he didn't look much like a big, bold, dark, scarred, adventurous pirate.

Tim grinned. "You always go for treasure. But what's treasure and pirating got to do with Newfoundland? Or are you just making things up?"

14

"This place was just full of pirates long ago. Of course I'm not making things up. Pirates, and treasure. Not even so very long ago, maybe only about a hundred years ago. One very big treasure vanished then, the Cocos Island treasure, and a Newfoundland man took it. The Loot of Lima, they call it, capital letters, Tim. His name was Captain Thompson, and he got the treasure in Lima, Peru. It was put aboard his ship for safety because Peru was at war. Jeepers, Tim, listen . . . seventy million dollars' worth of gold, and maybe about a ton of things out of churches; crosses and statues and things, covered with jewels, and crowns and diamond necklaces and ruby rings bigger than your thumb. This Captain Thompson killed the mission fathers that were sent to guard the gold on his ship, and he escaped. Later on when they caught him he said it was hidden on Cocos Island. But when soldiers took him there to make him show where he had hidden it, he and a cabin boy got away. You know what I think? I think it never was on Cocos Island, I think he just brought it straight home to Newfoundland and hid it. And it must still be here, because nobody has ever found even a scrap of it."

"It sounds like a lot of stuff to try to hide, Mat. Where would he have hidden it, on this rocky island? A hundred years ago? Don't be so dumb. Where are you going to hide seventy million dollars' worth of gold so that nobody ever finds it?"

"Oh, I've got ideas," Mat said stubbornly. "There must have been lots of secret pirate hideaways here in New-foundland. There had to be. One special pirate, Sir Henry something-or-other with a long name, he came here a lot to hide and fix up his ship. He said, 'There is no spot in the world better than Newfoundland for an honest pirate to refit.' "

"Refit?" Tim repeated. And then, "An *honest* pirate?"

Mat glanced down at a page. "Refit means, they had to go somewhere to overhaul their boats every once in a while. This old Sir Henry, he used to hang around the Spanish Main and capture big tall Spanish ships loaded with gold and jewels. Then he would dash up here to get out of trouble and hide out for a while. I bet he left treasure here. He had a cave, it says, a cave so big he could sail his ship right into it and stay for two or three months, keeping out of sight — when things got too hot down on the Spanish Main and he didn't dare run for England."

"Where's the Spanish Main?"

"Well, I don't know exactly," Mat admitted. "I think it was the ocean around the West Indies. But that's maybe not right. Somewhere around the West Indies and South America, anyway. All that gold and stuff came from South America." He put the book down on his knee. His tip-tilted eyes were far away. "Nobody has ever found that cave, Tim."

"Well?"

"I bet he stored treasure in it. I bet he came back and forth from the Spanish Main to Newfoundland and hid the loot in his mammoth cave, maybe until he had a couple of tons of it. Then after a while he'd go back to England and sell it. But maybe he didn't take it all."

"Oh, phooey," Tim said. Mat liked the thought of lost treasure. He would probably be a geologist, like their father, who could find gold or uranium or silver and other precious metals when nobody else could. He and Tim had already

17

found all the treasure any kids were entitled to find, back in Ontario. They hadn't been able to keep a penny of it, because it had belonged to somebody else. But it had made a kind of miracle for them anyway.

"When was this special pirate around Newfoundland?"

"Oh, a long time ago. More than three hundred years."

"So, if he had such a big cave, somebody would have found it. And if he had left anything in it, a silly thing for a pirate to do, somebody would have taken that, donkey's years ago, too."

"Well," Mat said. He got up and put the book down. "I guess if it was such a very big cave . . ." He came and stood at the window, looking out at the shining water of the Narrows. "There sure has been a lot of history sailing in and out of there. You know the way I feel about Newfoundland?"

"Well, no, I guess I don't. Not exactly."

"Well," Mat said again, slowly. "It's not like part of the real world. It's off the edge, some way or another. It's — well, it's kind of magic. This book says that somebody or other named this part of it Avalon. That's King Arthur. I mean, Avalon is where King Arthur was buried. You see what I mean. King Arthur was a kind of magic. So anything can happen here. It's not a *real* place, that's what I'm trying to say."

"Oh, jeepers," Tim said. "Here we go again."

CHAPTER

2

THE PATTERSONS had three sets of cousins living in St. John's: the Merricks, the Crockers and the Kennedys. They weren't first cousins. It was pretty hard to know just what kind they were. Their mothers and fathers were cousins of Lucy Patterson, the children's mother. Mrs. Crocker was her cousin and Mr. Merrick was her cousin and Mrs. Kennedy's brother-in-law was her cousin, or something like that. It didn't matter. You called everybody by his first name, grownup or not, and it was very nice. Over on the mainland the Pattersons had no relatives at all.

Two of the Kennedy children, Jerry and Moira, were coming to the hotel this morning to take Meg, Tim and Mat down to get The Fish. This was a mysterious errand. "Ye'll come with us in the mornin' to get The Fish, now, surely?" Jerry had asked last night. "We'll come by about nine."

So they were all going to get The Fish, whatever that meant. There were far too many strangenesses in Newfoundland to puzzle out without asking questions ahead of time.

They all ate breakfast in the dining room, and then Mrs. Patterson and Meg took the twins back upstairs while Tim and Mat waited in the lobby. It was only quarter to nine. There weren't many other people staying in the hotel right now. There had been a lot of fog in the last ten days or so, and when Newfoundland was "fogged in" people didn't try to fly over from the mainland. The road to Port aux Basques, across the island, connecting with the ferry to Cape Breton, wasn't paved yet — not all the way. The road was rough and bumpy, so tourists hadn't started to swarm in. Maybe they never would; first it was a long, long way by ship from Cape Breton on the mainland to Port aux Basques and then more than five hundred miles across the Avalon Peninsula to St. John's.

There were four people who had been here when the Pattersons had arrived, five days ago. They had all left the dining room, and three of them were in the lobby now. Mr. Lewis Jones, a tall, silent, grey man with steely grey eyes and pale skin — a man who looked as if he always worked under artificial light — was standing in front of a window looking over a newspaper. Mr. Jones didn't talk to people. He didn't seem to know anybody. He ate all his meals alone in the dining room; he went out of the hotel every day on foot, so he must have business close by. But although the children had wondered a little about him in the few minutes they had away from their lively and busy cousins, they didn't know anything about him.

There were a man and his wife, who bothered Meg a good deal. The woman was little, as small as their own mother. She had very expensive clothes, Meg said. Meg wanted to be an artist, or a designer, and she always read all the fashion and art magazines she could get her hands on. Mrs. Manren's clothes were very fashionable. Today she had on a purple dress, or Tim decided it was a kind of purple. Her heels were so high he thought she would fall flat on her face every time she took a step, but she didn't. She glittered, too. She had about five rings and she always wore at least two bracelets, and earrings and brooches and whatever else you could think of. Meg watched to see what different kinds she had. Today, as she left the boys to go upstairs with her mother and the twins, Meg muttered under her breath, "Amethysts and diamonds. Yesterday it was emeralds and sapphires."

Mr. Manren was a lot older than his wife, old enough to be her father. He was tall. He wasn't exactly fat, but you always got the feeling he was holding his stomach in. He was as bald as an egg, and he had dark puffs under his small brown eyes. He was very proud of his wife; he watched her all the time, and he didn't seem to like it if she talked to any other men. There wasn't anybody else much for her to talk to right now — Mr. Lewis Jones probably didn't even know she was alive, and there weren't any other men around except Mr. Dick Ackley. Mr. Dick Ackley was very friendly; he would talk to anybody and everybody at the drop of a hat. He had talked to the children a great deal, telling them interesting things about Newfoundland. He was writing a book. He had a rented car, and he drove all over the island, getting stories and all kinds of

21

information for his book. He could answer just about any question Mat wanted to think up, and that was saying a good deal.

Mr. Manren had been buying a box of expensive cigars at the newsstand. Mrs. Manren was picking out the newest and most expensive magazines. They must be rich. They had the biggest and shiniest station wagon Tim had ever seen. They had come from Cape Breton by ferry and had driven across from Port aux Basques. Mrs. Manren said she had never seen Newfoundland before and she just loved new, exciting places. Meg had heard her say it. Up in the Patterson's living room yesterday, Meg had said, "What's so exciting to *her* about Newfoundland? You'd think she'd want to go to Paris. She hasn't even been to any of the Handicraft places, not even the Nurses' Outport Shop, Nonia. She hasn't got a single Newfoundland thing. She probably wouldn't wear anything from Newfoundland."

Mrs. Patterson had said, "Maybe she's having things knitted or woven specially for her, Meg. Nonia takes orders. How do you know she hasn't been in there?"

"Because I asked them. Mom, you know what lovely things they've got. Sweaters and skirts and scarves and everything that the Outport women make. They *need* to sell them. Mrs. Manren's got so much money, I thought that surely she'd have gone to buy lots of these lovely things. I think I'll ask her — maybe she hasn't heard anything about Nonia."

"Meggie," Mrs. Patterson said firmly, "you mind your own business. I don't think Mrs. Manren would like having you make suggestions about her clothes, I really don't."

Tim and Mat sat now on a leather couch in the lobby,

23

waiting for Meg to come back and waiting for it to be nine o'clock. Mr. Dick Ackley, coming up the stairs from the street level, saw them. He came over and dropped down into a chair facing them. He had been out already. He always got up early, he had told them, to catch worms. Grinning, he said, "So, what are your plans for today? Who's coming to get you to do what?"

Mr. Dick Ackley had dark, wise, glinting eyes. He was always asking questions. Of course, that was his business. Writers had to learn things.

Tim said easily, "We don't exactly know." Tim didn't like questions too much.

Mat glanced at him. Mat said, "What he means is, we don't exactly understand. Jerry and Moira Kennedy, our cousins, are coming in a few minutes to take us to get The Fish. What fish? Where? We don't know. And then at eleven o'clock, all three families of our cousins are coming to take us troutin'. What's troutin'?"

Mr. Ackley got out a battered package and lit a cigarette. "I can see your difficulties," he said. "So the Kennedys are coming to take you to get The Fish? That's simple enough. Kennedy. Irish. Catholics, no doubt. And it's Friday. Simple."

"Is it?"

"Oh, very. You see, Wednesdays and Fridays are fast days, no meat for good Catholics; so at least one or two trawlers make a point of coming in here to the foot of the street, to the wharf below Water Street. The fishermen bring the fresh fish ashore. And the children of the families go down to get the day's supply. Get it?"

"Well, fine," Mat said. "In a way. And what's troutin'?"

24

"Troutin', my boy, is trouting. It means you're going fishing for trout — out to a lake, or as they always call it here, a pond. Seems that long ago, back in Devon, where a great many of these people came from, the word was pond. So a lake here is a pond. There are trout in a pond, and you go troutin' in a pond. Which pond are you going to?"

"We don't know," Tim said again, flatly.

"Why don't they call it going fishing?" Mat demanded. "Isn't that what it is?"

"No, it isn't. The only fish in these waters, inland or offshore, my interested young friend, is cod. You go *fishing* for cod. For any other fish, no! You go for the salmon in the rivers or you go troutin' in a pond. Am I clear?"

Mat stood looking at him. He said, "I guess it's kind of history, isn't it?"

"You are *so* right. Cod was the only reason for Newfoundland about four hundred years ago. Cod *was* Newfoundland. You know what? Queen Elizabeth the First was so anxious to get revenue from the Newfoundland fishermen that she passed a law saying people had to eat no meat, only fish — codfish — at least one day a week." He laughed. "Don't get me started again on Newfoundland history. You'll be so drenched in it that all next year in school you won't be able to see anything that ever happened in the Old World or America, without thinking of Newfoundland." He crushed out his cigarette. "By the way, who are all these cousins of yours?"

Meg had come from the elevator. She looked from Tim to Mat to Mr. Ackley. Tim wasn't answering. Mat was hesitating. Meg said easily, "The Kennedys and the Crockers and the Merricks. They're our mother's cousins."

25

He raised his eyebrows. "Crockers and Kennedys and Merricks. You know the old rhyme? Crockers and Crewes and Coplestone, when the Conqueror came, were already at home. Which was your mother, a Crocker or a Kennedy or a Merrick?"

"None of those," Meg said. "Her name was Lucy Vaughan."

"Vaughan," Dick Ackley repeated. "The head of one of the first big colonies in Newfoundland was a Vaughan. A Welshman. Related, like all the other early Newfoundlanders, to Raleigh and Drake and Gilbert and Grenville and Frobisher and the other great adventurers. The people here don't know their heritage, but that's what it is. I fell into knowing that. I'm a distant relative myself, very distant. And I'll tell you something I find exciting — you can look it up, prove it, when you go home. Try the *Encyclopedia Britannica,* for one thing. These people are all cousins. The great adventurers were all cousins, through one family — the Carews. Strongest and toughest blood in the world, if you can call blood tough. You want to know why?"

"Why?" Mat said.

"Well, because they're Norman-Welsh. I'll give you a short history. What happened when the Saxons overran England? You must know. The softies gave in and accepted Saxon rule. The tough dark people, the real Britons, they were too few to defeat the Saxon hordes, so they kept moving west. They're the Welsh. They stayed tough and hard to beat. So when William the Conqueror took England, he sent his toughest and strongest Norman barons over there to the Welsh marches to try to wipe out the

26

unruly Welsh. It never succeeded, never. Living close together, the Welsh and the Normans were always capturing each other's beautiful maidens and marrying them. And one great Norman called Gerald married a beautiful Welsh princess called Nest, the daughter of King Griffith. She married several other people in her lifetime. One set of her children were Fitz-Geralds, and another were Carews. And their descendants were Sir Walter Raleigh and Sir Humphrey Gilbert and Sir Francis Drake and all the others. Cousins. The ancestors of Newfoundland." He grinned at Meg. "So in a way, Meg, you're a princess. How do you like the idea?"

She crinkled her eyes at him. "I love it," she said. "Who wouldn't?"

CHAPTER

3

JERRY KENNEDY was Mat's age, eleven, and he had red hair and so many freckles you couldn't see any skin between them. Moira was a year older, with black curly hair and dark blue eyes. They were waiting at the street door outside the hotel at nine o'clock. Maybe they had never been in the hotel. Well, Tim decided, the Pattersons had never lived in a hotel before; he might have felt a little queasy about walking boldly into the Royal York, for instance, back home in Toronto, or the King Edward. You didn't know what to do in a big hotel until you had stayed in one.

"So — it's ready y'are," Jerry said. "Come along, then. It's not a far way." He led them down the slope toward the wharf, where the blue water glinted in the sun. They were facing Signal Hill. Away up on the top, Cabot Tower sat

28

like a stone watchman staring out over the Atlantic. Jerry saw Tim's glance. He said, "It's up the hill you've been, now, surely? Ivrywan goes up the hill, first off. Me dad says they ought to have a turnstile, like, and collect a few pennies for widdies and orphans." He wrinkled up his nose. "That's me dad's joke, Tim, our widdies and orphans gets their pay from Canada every month."

Moira said in her soft voice, "Don't be braggin', now, Jerry boy. Widdies and orphans in Canada gets their pay, too. Don't they, Meg?"

"Well," Meg said, trying to think, "I don't know. I never thought much about it. But *this* is Canada. So I suppose everybody gets the same."

"Canada?" Jerry said, stopping to look at her. "This was niver Canada, girrl. This is Newfoundland."

"Never mind," Tim said quickly. His father had explained a few things to him when they had first arrived. Newfoundland had been the very first English Colony in the whole world, and for four and a half centuries she had been away off here in the Atlantic, sitting proud and alone. But the going had got too rough, and finally Newfoundland had had to join Canada. Plenty of Newfoundlanders, his father said, would rather have joined the United States. But their loyalty to the British Crown, the British flag and the British Commonwealth of Nations had brought them to join Canada. They hadn't really wanted to join with anybody; it was very hard on their pride not to be able to be independent. Tim said, still gazing up at Signal Hill towering against the sky above the Narrows, "Dad drove us up there the first day we came. He said it was the closest point to Europe from anywhere in America."

29

"Well, to be sure," Jerry said proudly.

Moira was walking a little ahead, going down the steep slope. She turned. "You'd all be knowin' about Marconi, then?"

Mat said softly, "Well, to be sure we know about Marconi. There's a great big iron ring up there on the hill, fastened into a stone block. Dad said Marconi must have tied his kite to that ring when he sent it up to catch the first wireless signals from Ireland. Or was it Cornwall? To be sure, we know."

Moira looked at him suspiciously to see whether he was mocking Jerry, but Mat's eyes always looked as innocent as a day-old kitten's. Tim said firmly, "There's lots we don't know, though. We don't know exactly where we're going right now."

"Ye don't?" Jerry said, astonished. "Why, we're goin' down to the wharf to get The Fish. It's two twenty-five-cent fish me mother said I was to buy. See, I've got the money." He showed two silver quarters clutched in his hand. "We're goin' to give you fish 'n brewis fer yer lunch today, goin' troutin'. Anyways, we always goes to get The Fish on Fridays and Wednesdays. What else is there to do? Don't you go to get The Fish at home?"

"We haven't got anywhere to go," Meg said. "We haven't got any fish to speak of." She waved a hand around at the scurrying street. "Are all these children going down to get The Fish too?"

"Well, to be sure," Mat said quickly. "What else?"

Tim edged over to Mat. "You shut up," he said.

Mat looked at him out of his tip-tilted, fun-making eyes. "Oh, all right," he said. "All right!"

30

They had come to a street running parallel to the sea, Water Street. The first and oldest street in St. John's. It was broad and clean now, and paved, lined with neat shops. Big Ben Patterson had said that long ago Water Street had been a narrow lane, with wide shelves built out overhead for drying fish. It hadn't really been a street at all, just a sort of passageway. And even a few years ago, it had still been cobbled, with big round boulders that made walking and driving dangerous and bumpy. Tim found himself thinking that he would have liked to see this oldest city in North America long, long ago. The oldest English city in North America; a city begun only a few years after Columbus had made his first landfall in the West Indies.

Water Street was crowded with children, boys and girls about eight or ten years old. Moira explained. "It's the youngest who have to go get The Fish," she said. "We've all to take our turns, you might say. It's a thing you get a bit weary of, gettin' up in the early mornin' and scramblin' down the hill to get The Fish, when it's foggy and cold and maybe the trawler couldn't get in anyways. But it's got to be done. In our fam'ly, Jerry's turn has come. I had mine. So he's got the money, an' it's his job now."

Jerry turned abruptly into a wide gateway and began to walk down over a planked wharf. The water was only a short distance below them now. Gathered together in a huddle at the foot of the short street were a lot of small boats, empty. On the planking of the wharf, three or four roofed-over stalls had been built. Each one had a wide counter, with one or two men behind it. Children crowded around the counters, holding up money. The men turned, reached into tubs behind them, brought out shining big-

31

headed silvery fish and slapped them one by one down on the counter. One small boy, surely not more than six, got a fish almost as tall as he was. He dropped it to the wharf, unfolded a newspaper he had been carrying, rolled the fish in it and staggered off up the hill, clutching the fish to him as if it were a baby. Jerry, too, had a folded paper under his arm. He pushed his way to the counter and slapped down his money. "It's two twenty-five-cent fish I'll be wantin'," he said.

The man behind his counter was young, dressed in an old blue shirt and faded overalls. "Sure, two twenty-five-cent fish, lad," he replied, and brought them out. Jerry dropped them to the wharf and started to roll them in his paper. They were big — they were about a yard long, each of them, with big ugly heads, and heavy. Tim and Mat both started forward. Tim got to Jerry first. "I've never carried a fish," he said, "I've never even seen a fish as big as that, close up. Let me carry one of them?"

Jerry had struggled to his feet with the two enormous codfish wrapped in the newspaper; he could hardly see over them. "Well, if ye put it that way," he said. "I might do with a bit of a hand." He dropped the parcel to the wharf, unrolled it, and Tim wrapped one of the fish, slippery and awkward, and struggled up with it.

Meg said, "Why don't they all bring baskets, or bags, or something?"

Moira looked at her with her dark eyes. "Baskets?" she said. "Bags?"

"Wouldn't it be easier?"

"Easier?" Moira repeated. She looked around at the children puffing up the hill, each one clutching a big, slippery,

heavy fish. She said in a helpless voice, "It's how we've done it, this way."

They went on back up to the hotel. Jerry and Moira lived only two blocks farther on. "We'll be back at eleven to take you troutin'," Moira said. "Never mind a thing about boots and the like. We've collected them for you."

"Boots?" Meg said. "What kind of boots?"

"Well, ye'd get nowheres without boots," Moira said kindly. "It's across the marsh we've got to go, to get to the pond. We've got boots and long warm trousers for the three of you, and jackets and caps. The wind blows fierce, up on the marsh. Dad and Hughie Crocker and Tom Merrick, they've got the fishin' rods and the worms for bait. You don't need to think of a thing. Just be ready to go at eleven, if that's all right."

The three Pattersons stood in the hotel doorway and watched Jerry and Moira trudge off; Jerry was clutching both the big fish, but the street was nearly level here and he hadn't far to go. Meg, watching them, said slowly, "I'm going to talk to Mom. It seems to me that we could buy a piece of heavy plastic and make a long bag, like a golf bag, with a strap to go over Jerry's head. Then he could slide the fish into the bag and hang it down his back."

Mr. and Mrs. Manren came out of the hotel. Their emperor-size station wagon was parked at the curb. Mrs. Manren had her elaborate camera. She saw Jerry trudging up the street, laughed scornfully and took a picture of him. Other children were making their way up the slope, facing her, with the big fish clasped in their arms. She took more pictures. "It's simply unbelievable," she said. "I don't understand it. Why doesn't somebody have a fish truck and take

34

the fish around to the people's houses? Why don't they pack fish in ice and sell them the way civilized people sell fish?"

The three Pattersons stood looking at her, not saying anything. Meg's mouth had a tight look. Mat's eyes were quiet. Tim was angry inside, but he didn't know why.

"Oh, well," Mrs. Manren said. She walked toward the front seat of the station wagon. She was carrying a purple bag to go with her dress. Her rings had stones as big as lighthouse lamps, and her bracelets had stones much bigger than the jewels Mat and Tim had found in the long-lost box in Echo Valley. Mr. Manren looked fancy, too; he had on a pale-grey city suit, with a silk shirt and shiny city shoes. They were both much too dressed-up for Newfoundland.

Mr. Manren said carelessly, "We're off on a sightseeing trip. Some of the Outports."

"Yes, with their ridiculous names," Mrs. Manren said. She shut the door and turned down the glass of her window. "Heart's Delight, and Tickle Cove Pond, and Cupids', and Portugal Cove, and Goblin! I'm going to take dozens of pictures. Nobody in New York will believe me unless I do."

Mr. Manren got in. The oversized car slid away from the curb. The three children stood looking after it. "That car would look real nice stuck in about three feet of marsh," Mat said thoughtfully.

CHAPTER

4

Mrs. Patterson hadn't yet left to go to the Crockers when the children went upstairs to their hotel sitting room. She was dressing the twins in shorts and shirts for a day of play with the little Crockers. She looked neat and pretty in a yellow cotton dress, plain, without any jewels or foolish high heels. She looked younger than Mrs. Manren, too, Tim decided, with her fair hair trying to curl in little wisps around her head and her face almost always happy and calm again after the long year when they had worried every minute because their father was missing. She had a little frown now, though. There was something she had made up her mind to say.

Then she said it.

"You three are going to have a new adventure today," she began. "I want you to promise me one thing: that

36

whatever happens, you'll stay together. All three of you. I know I can trust you when you're together. Meg has a lot of responsibility for fourteen, and Tim is wonderful in any emergency, and Mat is pretty bright about seeing around a situation. There will be eleven children going today, and three men. Meg is the oldest of the children except Shannie Kennedy, and even Shannie is only sixteen. So you must promise me to stay together, except, of course, when you are in the cars. They will want to divide you up, on the drive, to have new people to talk to. Promise?"

Mat said, "What's there to be scared of, Mom?"

She shook her head. "I don't know. Newfoundland is beautiful. Just look out there at the water in the sunshine, and the cliffs, and the power and awe of Signal Hill — it's beautiful. I love Newfoundland. But it can be very cruel and very dangerous and very unexpected. It's not a bit like the mainland, not a bit like home. I don't *know* what could happen. I never lived on this side of the island, I lived in Cornerbrook, away on the other side, facing the mainland. It's different — not so exposed, somehow."

"But we're only going to a pond, not very far off the road," Tim said. He didn't like his mother to worry. "And there will be three men, Newfoundlanders, who know their way around. What on earth could happen?"

"I don't know, dear. I just don't know. But all my young life there were always stories of boats disappearing at sea, never heard of again, sealing ships cracking up in the ice, children wandering into the back country and never found. It's a very big island, and very lonely."

Mat said with his grin, "She's thinking about pirates. A whole shipload will come crawling up a gully from the

37

ocean with knives in their teeth and steal us away for ransom. That's what will happen."

"Pirates?" his mother repeated. "Who put that nonsense into your mind?"

"Well, it's in books. But Mr. Dick Ackley told us first."

"Mr. Dick Ackley talks too much. There aren't any pirates, of course there aren't. There aren't even —" she stopped. She laughed. "You know, long ago, maybe three hundred years ago, the Yankee traders from New England used to come and steal our boys and men, and take them off to Boston or Philadelphia as indentured servants, not much better than slaves. It wasn't actually stealing; the Yankee traders were merchants, and they sailed around from one Outport to another, selling Yankee goods — mostly rum, I am afraid. The Outport people would get so far in debt they could never pay in money, and they used to have to sell themselves, in a way, to pay off the debt. They'd go to New England to work off a debt and maybe they did pay it and maybe they didn't, but many of them never came back. Of course, life was easier in New England and maybe they didn't want to come back. But Newfoundland remembers lots and lots of lost men and boys — vanished, gone. They say that sometimes the Yankee traders nailed them up in big casks to keep anyone from knowing they were being taken away, willingly or not."

Tim went into his and Mat's bedroom, opening off the sitting room. "I'm taking my Boy Scout stuff," he said. "A knife and a compass and a flashlight. Maybe I better take my hatchet, too, in case we get nailed up in a cask. Shall I, Mom?"

"Oh, don't be silly," she said, and laughed again. "I'm just trying to say — well, that I've got hidden fears in my mind and of course I *am* silly. Hughie Crocker is a schoolteacher, as responsible and sensible as any man I ever knew. Tom Merrick has a big store, but he's spent every free minute fishing and hunting and he has lived here all his life and knows Newfoundland like the palm of his hand. As for Pat Kennedy, his father was a fisherman, and Pat grew up in an Outport and knows the sea like a book. They wouldn't take their own children or you to any place where there was danger. But you will promise to stay together?"

"We always do," Mat said gently.

She put her arm around him and hugged him. "Yes, of course. You always do. So it's all right."

❊ ❊ ❊

When the cars came, Meg was to ride with the Crockers because the three Crocker boys, Paul, Jamie and Ricky, didn't have a sister and they'd appreciate one, Hughie Crocker said. He was a small man with glasses, wiry and quick in his movements. Mat was to go with Pat Kennedy and Jerry and Moira and Shannie. And Tim was invited into the Merrick car, with big Tom Merrick hunched over the wheel because he was so tall. His children were Gilly, twelve, and Emmy and Dierdre, nine and ten. With two fairly small girls, Tom Merrick said, he needed another big boy to keep them straight.

The first part of the road was paved. They drove a long way, with Pat Kennedy leading the procession. Tim was glad to be in the last car; he could keep an eye on the two ahead, and in a way make sure that he and Meg and Mat were really all together and staying that way. There wasn't going to be any danger, but they *were* heading for the wilderness.

They turned off on a gravelled road, dusty and bumpy,

and drove along that for another long time. Tim was beginning to feel really hungry. Then, suddenly, he saw Pat Kennedy's car ahead pull over to the side of the road in what looked like a sort of park, with lots of trees and among them, wooden tables and benches. It was a pleasant place, although the trees weren't big and shady; none of the trees around St. John's was big, like the evergreens at home. But beside the road was something you'd never see at home — a stone thing almost like a shrine, built into the side of the steep hill. It was topped with a stone cross, and beneath the cross, inside the shrine, a stream of icy water ran out of the rock.

"Father Duffy's Well," Tom Merrick said. "A travelling priest found it long ago, a little flowing well of good water, and later on it was enclosed this way. It's safe water. So this was made into a picnic ground."

The picnic was a queer meal. At home there would have been sandwiches, and milk in thermos bottles, and maybe big juicy tomatoes and a lot of fruit. That was what a Patterson picnic would have been in Echo Valley or up in Muskoka. But tomatoes and fruit in this part of Newfoundland were worth their weight in rubies because they had to be flown in from Halifax or Montreal. As for milk, the Patterson's had already sadly found out about milk. Each of them drank at least a quart a day at home. There wasn't that much milk to be had in St. John's. People used powdered milk, not really very tasty to drink.

Meg helped Shannie Kennedy and the three men set the table and made lunch. Tom Merrick put a two-burner gas stove on a big flat rock. "We can't build campfires here, it's against the law," he explained. "We have to save our forests

40

if we can." He lit the stove. Gilly Merrick had carried a pail of water up from Father Duffy's Well, and Paul Crocker did too. Shannie filled two big cooking pots with water. She put potatoes in one to boil, with a bowlful of pieces of fat salt pork. "Mind now," she said to Jerry and Moira, "you're not to eat the pork. It's Friday. Father McGrath won't say a word about the taste, but you're not to take even a wee nibble of the meat."

"They won't, girrl," her father said. He was unwrapping another bowl, and in it were the pieces of the two big cod-fish. The potatoes and salt pork were soon nearly cooked, and then into the pot went the pieces of fish. "It's not exactly the real thing," Pat Kennedy said when finally the food was cooked and served in bowls on the table. "Fish 'n brewis, that's made wid ship's biscuit, hardtack ye might call it, soaked in salt water and cooked in wid de fish. That's what the fishermen eat in their dories, early in the mornin' after they've been sittin' all night, like, jiggin' for cod or puttin' out nets and then draggin' thim in. It's hard work. So they make a wee fire on board, on a few bricks or stones right on the boat, and cook up a kettle of fish 'n brewis, and then dump it out on a board athwart de gunnels, and everybody dips in. They calls it a mug-up. With big mugs of strong tea, full o' sugar, it's a meal to put heart into a tired man. Mind ye, lots o' times nowadays they takes along potatoes instead o' hardtack, so in a way, this is near enough fish 'n brewis, the national dish of Newfoundland." He didn't say "with," he said "wid," and he didn't always say "the," sometimes he said "de." It was fun listening to him.

"Well, it's *good*," Meg said. She held out her bowl. "May I have a little more, Shannie?"

"Oh, it's more than welcome you are," Shannie said. Her round face was happy. Maybe she had been afraid at first of Meg, a city girl from the mainland, even if they were cousins; but she wasn't afraid now. She spooned out a good helping into Meg's bowl. "Come along, now then, lads, don't let your sister be puttin' you to shame. Here, hold out the bowls."

Mat was sitting with his spoon in his hand, thinking. Tim felt uneasy. Mat would think of almost anything and say it, too. But he was only going over the rhyme that Dick Ackley had told them. He said, " 'Crockers and Crewes and Coplestone, when the Conqueror came, were already at home.' What does that mean, Hughie?"

"What did you say, now?" Hugh Crocker asked, surprised. "It's not a thing I ever heard. Give it me again, lad."

Mat repeated the rhyme. Hughie Crocker took his glasses off and polished them. He said, "Now, where would you be picking up a thing like that? I never heard it in all my life, and I'm a Crocker."

"A man at the hotel is writing a book," Mat explained. "Dick Ackley. He told it to us this morning."

Meg took a drink of her hot tea. "I think he knows what he's talking about. 'When the Conqueror came' — that must be William the Conqueror. And doesn't the rhyme mean that the Crockers and the Crewes and the Coplestone families were already at home in England when he came? That's a long, long time ago. That's nine hundred years ago! And they must be awfully important families, mustn't they, to have such long records?"

Hughie Crocker stared at her. "Crockers? Crewes? Important? Oh, no. Ordinary Newfoundlanders. We're on our way to Crewes' Pond right now. That's where we go

43

troutin'!" His eyes were interested. "I'd like a good long talk with your Dick Ackley man," he said. "It's likely that he knows things about our people here that we don't know ourselves. We were never important. We know we're descended from the humble hard-working folk of Devon. From poor fishermen. They came early, a bold lot, and they did great harm to Newfoundland, even if I do say it, a Devon man myself. They wanted to keep Newfoundland only for fishing, and they got rich at it. They didn't allow settlers in here, not for a long time."

Mat said slowly, "Sir Walter Raleigh was from Devon."

"That's true, lad. You'd have had him in your mainland history too? He was a great lad. I think Newfoundland was his dream. I've been doing a bit of digging in history, too, and I think Sir Walter Raleigh was responsible for Newfoundland, in a way."

Pat Kennedy grinned. He said, "Ye've set off a trigger, bhoy. Hughie here's always talkin' about that wan, to be sure."

"Well, it's a thing we should know more about," Hughie said. "You see, our first governor, around about 1618, was Sir Humphrey Gilbert. Now, he was a half-brother to Sir Walter Raleigh. He was fourteen years older. Maybe the younger lad made a sort of an idol out of him. But there's more — it's a bit of odd history. But it starts at Oxford University, believe it or not. Raleigh went to Oxford. Sir Humphrey Gilbert went to Oxford, a bit earlier. William Vaughan, who brought our first lot of settlers, was an Oxford man, a bit later than Gilbert but about the same time as Raleigh. Captain John Mason, who came to Newfoundland in the same year, was an Oxford man. Sir Henry

44

Cary, Lord Falkland, who brought early settlers, was educated at Oxford, same years. George Calvert, Lord Baltimore, who was here during the early days and then went to Maryland, was at Oxford with the others. Sir Henry, our gentleman pirate, was likely also at Oxford. You see what I'm saying, lads? These youngsters going up to Oxford at fourteen or fifteen, sat around talking together back in the middle of the 1500's, and what did they talk about? Newfoundland! They were young and full of life and spirit, and it was only fifty years and a bit since Columbus had discovered America and Cabot had got to Newfoundland. Fishermen were already coming to Newfoundland. What more likely than that these boys set their hearts on Newfoundland and determined to explore it? Mind you, this was many years before the Mayflower went to Salem, down in Massachusetts. That was a brave bold lot of boys. You see what can come out of the minds of bright schoolboys when they churn things over?" He took a deep breath. "It's a pity they didn't come to settle themselves here and raise families. Newfoundland might never have gone through such bad times if we'd been made of their fine noble blood."

"But Dick Ackley says you *are* of their fine noble blood," Meg said. She told them the things Dick Ackley had said that morning; of the Normans and the Welsh and the princess who was the mother, in a way, of all the great Elizabethan adventurers. Shannie listened with shining eyes. Hugh Crocker was frowning, interested but not quite believing. The others didn't really care.

It was Mat who got down to business. When Mat had an idea in his head he kept it there. He said, "Sir Walter Raleigh did come here to live for a while, didn't he? Dick

45

Ackley said the other day that he came to Newfoundland with a whole boatload of gold from — well, from some South American river —"

"The Orinoco?" Hughie shook his head. "It's doubtful if he came with any gold, my lad. He'd gone looking for his Eldorado. He was not in the great Queen's esteem; had he found his gold, he'd have taken it to her, surely. As for living here or bringing good men to live here, it seems unlikely. It's said that on that last voyage of his he had to man his ships with the scum of the earth; he was disgraced, and nobody else would sail with him." He said thoughtfully, "But, on the other hand, Sir Humphrey Gilbert was here a long time — Sir Walter Raleigh's half-brother. Had he brought relatives to settle, and was Raleigh anxious to call in here on that trip, the only chance he'd had, to see how they were succeeding? Could that be true?"

"I could ask, now," Pat Kennedy said, "if the noble Sir Henry, the bold pirate, had any connection with Raleigh and Gilbert and the rest? He was the one took the governor on board his ship for a great feast — sick he was of associatin' with riffraff, he said, and the governor was a gintleman like himself. Was it Gilbert, then, that he took wantin' company? Maybe Sir Henry himself was wan of the bhoys, ye might say. He brought the governor back and no harm done, as if they could have been friendly, like. There was plenty of sinful pirates that took men off the island and niver brought them back, needin' hands to sail the ships and help with their cutthroat work."

"Sir Henry?" Mat repeated slowly. He was thinking again about that big cave. "He came here a lot, didn't he?"

"Yiss, indade, and he was a wan, he was. But we had all

46

kinds. We'd every brand of pirate ye might name, Portuguese and Spaniards and French, and plenty of English. Maybe even an Irishman or two, although I niver heard of wan. But I'd niver deny it. Newfoundland bein' off the beaten track, ye might say, they sneaked up here in the fog to get out of trouble. Oh, we had a great catch o' pirates, long and long ago."

Mat took a long drink of water. "Didn't some of them leave their treasure here? Has any ever been found?"

It was Tom Merrick who answered in his slow, careful way. "It's never been much talked about, lad. But there's been a good few people leave Newfoundland with riches. Nobody ever knew how they got the riches. You can't ever put your finger on any one story and prove it. Talk, mostly, I think. But the talk's there."

"What would happen to a pirate's treasure trove?"

Meg laughed. "Tim and Mat are treasure hunters," she explained. "They found treasure once, they probably think they can do it again." She told the story of the lost treasure, while they all finished their tea. Everybody sat very still and listened. "So that's it," Meg finished. "That's why Tim asks what would happen to a pirate's treasure trove. What would happen, Hughie?"

"What would happen?" he repeated. He got up and began to gather dishes together. Shannie got up too and brought the dishpan from the rock beside the stove, to fill it with water from a steaming kettle. "What would happen?" Hughie said again. "Well, it would belong to the government, surely. I should think so. But . . . if anybody were to find a pirate treasure . . . I doubt very much if he'd tell. He'd have to keep very, very quiet, and dip into it bit by bit, and

47

get it out of the country bit by bit. If it was once around that he'd found it, everybody and his old grey mare would be in there trying to get part of it. No, I'd say it would belong to the government, but how they'd get it is another matter."

"They need it," Pat Kennedy said. "Our Joey, now, if he could get his hands on pirate treasure, he'd spend it on roads. An' schools, an' new business, and dentists, and all kinds o' things we need, here in Newfoundland."

Tom Merrick said slowly, "The government nowadays isn't just Newfoundland, Pat. It's Canada. We joined Confederation. We're part of Canada, you remember that, lad?"

Pat stood still, with the teapot in his hands. "What kind of blasphemy is that? A pirate treasure hid away in Newfoundland for three — four hundred years, and we have to give it to Canada? Not by a long shot, we don't. It's ours!"

Hughie Crocker laughed. "Come along with you both, now," he said. "There'll be no troutin' today if we don't get on the road. Pirate gold, you're ready to fight about? Don't be foolish, lads. Come along."

CHAPTER
5

THEY DROVE for almost an hour after they left Father Duffy's Well. There was no kind of building or landmark where they stopped; no signpost or pointer, not even a path going off the road. But the men knew where to stop. They got out and began taking high rubber boots and heavy trousers and waterproof jackets from the cars, and everyone pulled on the extra clothing. Here on the road the sun was hot, and it seemed silly to be dressing for winter.

"I guess they know what they're doing," Mat said dryly to Tim. "Or what *we're* doing."

When everyone was dressed and the fishing rods handed out so that each person had one — even little Emmie and Dierdre, who said they had been troutin' dozens of times — the procession set out, across the road and up a long slope. The climb was easy enough, over rocky ground but on a kind of path. The heavy rubber boots, hip high, made the going slow, and there didn't seem to be much sense in wearing them; why not wait until they got to the lake, or pond, to put them on? But once at the top of the hill, Tim saw the reason for the boots. Here they were, on the top of the island, on what should have been solid rock. Down in St. John's, all over the Avalon Peninsula, people said there wasn't enough soil to grow gardens, certainly not enough for pasture. There was nothing but bare rock. But this was a marsh, growing thick with little flowers and bushes and vegetation that seemed to go away down in the wet soil. When you put your foot down it sank into the soggy earth. Walking was anything but easy. Tim, near the end of the procession, watched the men up ahead, plodding along steadily, taking this kind of walking for granted, but sinking halfway to their knees at every step. The little girls got along best; they didn't sink nearly so far. Mat was light, too, and he and Jerry Kennedy seemed to be able to skim along on the surface about as well as the little girls. But Shannie and Gilly and Paul, Tim and Meg kept sinking away down in the soft, treacherous marsh.

The wind up here was wild. It was cold, almost bitter.

Meg stopped, and Tim caught up with her. She was puffing, and her cheeks were pink. "This makes me think of the Grimpen Mire," she said. "You know, the Hound of the Baskervilles. How do the men know where they're going? There isn't any real path, just a kind of a faint track that keeps filling in. How do they know we won't walk right into a great big mire and sink all the way down?"

As if he had heard her, Pat Kennedy stopped and stepped aside to wait. Meg and Tim caught up with him. He said,

"The pond's not far ahead — fifteen minutes, no more. Ye'll soon get a glint of it." He looked at Meg sympathetically. "It's not aisy goin', girrl, is it?"

"It scares me," Meg said frankly. "I feel as if I'm going to sink down about a mile."

"Well, to tell ye the truth," he said, "it's possible that you might, at that. But not if ye folly the path. I niver heard of anywan sinkin', but nobody's walked over ivery foot o' this marsh. There's hundreds of miles of marsh on the island. If we could drain it, now, and use the land for hay or potatoes, we'd be a lot better off." He grinned at Tim. "You find that pirate treasure, lad, and our Joey'll find a way to drain the marshes, likely."

Meg had only heard part of what he said. "How can a person follow a path he can't see?" she asked.

"Well, there *is* a path, and we're on it. It fills in a bit, but when ye've walked this way a good few times, it's aisy. Except, of course, if the fog comes down." He glanced quickly up into the sky. "I couldn't find the path meself, if the fog was to come down. If ye're troutin' out at the pond and see a wisp o' fog, you make for the path and folly it fast to the road."

"Is there likely to be fog?" Tim asked carefully.

"That's no question to ask in Newfoundland, boy. Fog's a queer beast. Fog makes up its own mind. It can settle in so fast ye can't see yere hand in front of yere face, all in a second." He looked into the sky again, carefully. "There's no sign of it now. But I mind the time six of us was up here and the fog came, and we all had to yell ourselves hoarse, keepin' track o' each other and makin' our way back to the road. It wouldn't do to be lost up here in the marsh. When the fog comes down, there's no tellin' how long it will stay. It might lift in a minute, and it might not lift for a week or even two weeks." He turned and began to plod off again in the direction of the pond.

Meg said in a low voice, "I see what Mom meant."

Tim didn't answer. He was thinking that if the fog did come down, nobody could make any speed, trying to run back to the road on this path. Every footstep was a big struggle. And you wouldn't dare get off the path, such as it was, from what Pat said. There just might be places like the Grimpen Mire, where you could sink way down into it and be smothered. It wasn't a very nice thought.

Meg said, as if she had forgotten all about fog and mire, "There are a lot of beautiful little plants and flowers growing here."

Pat Kennedy turned. "That's the truth, girrl. The trouble is, we don't know what the half of thim are. Nobody's had time in Newfoundland to go into such things. But that little white flower — that's bake-apple, and there's partridge berry, and this brown thing is the pitcher plant, the emblem of Newfoundland. You know about the pitcher plant?"

"No."

"It eats things," he said. "There it sits, innocent as a baby, and when a poor helpless bug gets into the pitcher, sure it just swalleys that bug whole."

"The emblem of Newfoundland?" Meg repeated in a small voice. She took a deep breath. She glanced back over her shoulder toward the vanished road, the vanished cars and safety.

The pond wasn't a little shallow pond. It was a lake, a big one, with long arms stretching up and down a narrow gully. The wind was quieter once they got to the shore. Fishing was a lot of fun. It wasn't easy to cast out the lines, even when the wind had gentled, but when the bobber got any distance out from shore there were sure to be trout nibbling at the hook below. Most of them were little fish and had to be thrown back in; but Gilly Merrick caught one eight inches long, and Mat got one almost as big. Tim kept watching the others, keeping track of Meg and Mat. The men didn't go far away, up and down the shore, but they were so interested in fishing they didn't pay much attention to the children. They all stood out in the water in their hip boots, cast away out and reeled in. They weren't really afraid of Newfoundland; it was home to them, with its dangerous, boggy paths and its quick fogs. The Newfoundland children weren't afraid either, not even Emmie and Dierdre.

It was getting along toward evening; it was five o'clock when Hughie Crocker came wading along the shore and said, "I think we'd better start back. It's not good fishing anyway. I've only caught two. It's about two hours home, and there'll be four mothers waiting for their families." He put a hand to his mouth and called, and voices answered him all up and down the shore.

Tim reeled in his line for the last time, and he was glad they were going home. It was going to take twenty minutes or more to get back over that tricky path, and there was Mat to be thought of. Mat was having a wonderful time; he was farther away than anybody, away down the shore even beyond Jerry Kennedy. Tim called to him loudly, and at first Mat did not hear; then he waved a hand, and he began reeling his line in, too.

54

People started up toward the path from wherever they were on the shore. It was rocky for a hundred yards or so, and not dangerous. Meg hung back, waiting for Tim and Mat, but this was a single file path over the marsh and she had to go on. Mat was coming, with Jerry Kennedy and Jerry's father. Pat was watching over the boys, so it would be all right.

But it wasn't all right.

Nobody saw fog until they were in the middle of the marsh. Then, as if someone had suddenly lowered a thick white folded curtain, the fog was upon them. One minute you could see the soggy earth with the water standing in patches in the middle of the path, and the next, there was nothing. One minute you could see a line of people ahead, and the next, there was nobody; the world was empty.

Up ahead, Hughie Crocker called out loudly, "Stay in file, everybody! Don't lose the path! Come along with you, hurry as fast as you can. Stay in file!"

It wasn't possible to stay in file. It was only possible to plod along, hoping to stay on the path. Suddenly, right beside him, Tim found Tom Merrick standing and waiting. He said, "Good lad. You're doing fine. Go along with you, I'll wait for the others. There's four behind us but Pat's with them. Just keep going, lad, you're fine."

Tim went on, doing as well as he could. But he kept thinking of Mat, away behind him. He couldn't go on. He had to wait for Mat. He stood still, right in his tracks, and waited. At last he heard voices behind, Tom Merrick's reassuring voice and then Jerry Kennedy's and Gilly Merrick's, and finally Mat's. They sounded fine.

But the fog was much worse; moving ahead was like

groping through cotton batting. The earth underfoot was no path; it squelched and squished, and he kept stepping into puddles of water that shouldn't have been on the path at all. But the three men kept calling and calling, and the children answered cheerfully; it looked as if they might make the road after all.

At last, when it seemed as if he must have walked off the edge of the world, Tim stepped on rock again, and knew that he was at the top of the slope leading down to the road. It sounded as if Hugh Crocker, ahead, had got to the road. His voice was encouraging. Then Meg called out in her high, clear voice, "Tim! Mat! We're at the road! Where are you?"

Tim answered, and he thought he heard Mat's voice piping up behind him. He was almost sure he heard it. He went on. Hugh Crocker was saying, "Never mind your wet boots. Just pile into the cars. Get yourselves into the cars, quick. It'll be bad, slow driving. Come along, get in, all of you."

Car doors slammed, and slammed again. How many were up ahead? Hugh Crocker knew. And Tom Merrick, behind Tim, knew too, and Pat Kennedy was bringing up the rear. Everything was all right.

Tim got to a car. He said, "Meg?" But she didn't answer. He wouldn't get in. He went to the next car, and the next, and she was there, standing beside it on the road. "Meg?"

"Yes, I'm here," she said. Then, "Where's Mat?"

"He's coming. Pat Kennedy's bringing him. He's all right."

Tom Merrick came to them. "Get in, you two," he said. "Never mind which car. We've got to get moving." He opened the door. Meg got in, and Tim followed her; and then, in half a minute, without speaking, they both got out again. Mat hadn't got to the road yet. Or had he? Was he in one of the other cars?

They ran to the car ahead. Meg opened the door, said something, slammed the door again. Tim went past her, to the first car. Mat was not there.

He found Meg. They stood together waiting in the road. Tim said, "I bet he fell down. I bet he's beside the path. . . . Pat Kennedy likely walked right past him. . . ."

"Oh, no, no," Meg said. She raced up the rocky slope. There was nobody on it. "Mat, Mat!" she called.

Behind them on the road, everybody was shouting and climbing into cars and slamming doors. The men were counting noses. Tim heard somebody say, "Tim and Meg got into the Merrick car." He was about to turn and call when he heard, far up the slope, a faint voice — it was Mat. He knew it was Mat. He raced up the rocks toward it, and Meg was with him. They couldn't see each other; but they were together, and they knew it.

Mat was there, just as Tim had thought. He was off the path a yard or more, and he had stepped into a deep puddle and fallen. As they reached him, guided by his faint wavering voice, he was trying to lift himself from the marsh. His face was covered with mud; he had fallen face down. Tim and Meg each took an arm and lifted him. "Where's Pat Kennedy?" Tim demanded.

"He didn't know I fell," Mat said weakly. "I had a face full of mud. I couldn't say anything."

"Well, come on, quick," Tim said. "We can't keep them waiting. It's only a step or two to the rocky part, Mat. Come on, kid."

"Yes," Mat said dazedly, and took that last step or two. But just as he made it, the engines of all three cars started up. And, in about half a minute, they were all away. The cars were gone.

CHAPTER
6

PAT KENNEDY, driving the lead car back to town, said suddenly, "Who went wid Mat Patterson, Jerry? He was in the front of you all the way along the path. Why isn't he in the car here, boy?"

"He said he wanted to ride with Meg and Tim," Jerry said. "He said he promised his mother that they'd all stay together, Dad. He was callin' thim, the last bit."

*   *   *

Tom Merrick, in the second car, said, "Gilly, Meg and Tim got into this car — I opened the door for them myself. Did they get out again while I was stowing the gear in the back?"

"They went to ride in whatever car Mat was in," Gilly said. "They wanted to make sure he was O.K. He'd be with the Kennedys. We all come along the path together, me

59

and Mat just behind, and then Jerry and his father. So the Pattersons'll all be with the Kennedys."

*　*　*

Hugh Crocker said, "We've got Shannie Kennedy instead of Meg Patterson — where did Meg get to, Shannie?"

"Oh, she got into the Merrick car with Tim," Shannie said. "I heard Tom Merrick shut the door after them."

"And Mat?"

"He's with the Kennedys," said Paul and Ricky together. "He come up the path, Dad, with Jerry and Pat. We heard him."

*　*　*

Tim said steadily, "They'll soon find out we're not in the cars. They'll be back right away."

"We'd better get back down to the road," Meg said, in a voice that trembled a little. "Mat?"

"I've dropped my fishing rod," Mat said. "Just a minute. It's right here some place." He squelched off, a step or two. He squelched off again, a little farther. "I've got it," he said. "Where are you?"

Meg took a step toward his voice. "Come here, Mat. Come right here. We've got to get back to the road."

Tim put out a foot and felt for the rock. The fog was solid, so thick now you could cut it with a scissors. It was a good thing they were on the rock ledge, the ledge that sloped down to the road. If they'd been out in the marsh, even two yards out in the marsh, they wouldn't know which way to walk. He moved a few feet along the rock. It was firm underfoot. "Come on," he said.

He waited until the other two came to him. They joined hands. Mat hung on to his fishing rod. "All we have to do is go down the slope," Tim said. "Then when we get to the road, we're fine. They'll find out we're not in the cars. They'll be back any minute."

They groped foot by careful foot down the slope. It was slippery now; the dense fog was making the rocks wet. It was slow going. Every few steps they stopped, waiting, listening for the cars to come back. There was no sound of engines. There was nothing in the still, white world, nothing. No life, no sound, no movement, nothing but the terrible whiteness of the fog. They couldn't see each other's faces.

After a while Meg said, "I didn't know it was so far, Tim."

"Neither did I," Tim said slowly. "I think we'd better sit down. That's the rule. If you don't know exactly where you are, sit down and wait. They'll come back and find you."

Mat said in a low voice, "I don't think they'll come back. They won't miss us until they get all the way back to town. They'll think we're in some other car."

Tim didn't answer. Meg said slowly, "Tim, we got into the Merricks' car, remember? Tom Merrick put us in. And then we got out again. We didn't tell him we were getting out. Maybe he doesn't know we got out to look for Mat. When he finds out, he'll just think we got into whatever car Mat was in."

Tim sat down on a flat rock. "Come on," he said. "There isn't a thing to do but wait."

They waited. They waited for five minutes by Tim's watch. He could barely see it even with the flashlight. They waited for ten minutes, half an hour.

Meg said, "We've got to get back to the road, Tim. If we're on the road, we're safe. We can walk back toward

61

St. John's. We go to the left, that's all. We've just got to get back on the road!"

"Some other car might come along," Mat suggested. "It's cold, sitting here. There must be other cars that would go along that road!"

"Perhaps," Tim agreed doubtfully. "But we've got to hang on to each other. I'll go first."

He moved forward slowly, step by step. It was queer that they hadn't already come to the road; it hadn't been far from the top of the rocky slope. But they had been going down all the time, and the road had been downward. They couldn't miss it if they kept on going down. Could they?

After a long time, Meg said suddenly, 'We've come too far, Tim. I'm sure of it. We'd have come to the road long ago if we'd been going in the right direction."

Tim got out his compass and his flashlight. He had been thinking about them, but what good were they? He hadn't known what direction the road was from the marsh. That path had twisted and turned round on itself a dozen times, just as the road from St. John's had twisted and turned. The city might be north or south, he didn't know. He simply didn't know. But at least they could make a start from here. They needn't double back on their tracks, the way lost people did.

He looked at the compass hopelessly. "I still think we have to sit right here and wait," he said.

"Couldn't we find a pile of rocks?" Mat suggested. "The wind goes right through all these clothes. Meg's shivering and I'm freezing too. It's too cold, Tim. Let's find a pile of rocks, and then we can sit down on the side so the wind won't hit us."

"Well, all right," Tim said grudgingly. He knew it was wrong to move, but the wind was icy and growing stronger. Why didn't it blow the fog away? Was it because the whole world was full of fog? His mother was right. Newfoundland was a strange place, full of unknown dangers. It wasn't a bit like home. At home, if the wind blew as hard as this, the fog would vanish. Of course, there never was fog like this at home — nothing like this thick, white, solid stuff.

He moved slowly along the slippery rocks. He wasn't going to take one single step into the marsh. That meant awful trouble. It could mean . . . he stopped thinking about it. He suddenly wished for his father. Big Ben Patterson would know exactly what to do. Big Ben Patterson would never have got into a jam like this. He'd have used his head. He'd have made sure, back at the cars, that all three of them were together before the cars started, Tim told himself angrily. He should have said to Meg, we can't run back up that slope after Mat without telling anybody! It had been a crazy thing to do.

But it was done.

He didn't like leading them on and on, maybe farther and farther away from the road. What were the boundaries of the marsh? Maybe this rocky slope curved round and round it, maybe it went eventually right down to the sea. Maybe they were heading for the sea, not the road. How could he know?

It had taken the cars two hours to drive from St. John's, not counting lunch time, and in clear weather. It would take them three hours to get back to the city, for the men to find out that the Pattersons were missing; and then three more hours to come back, not counting time to buy gasoline and get organized. Seven hours! It had to be seven hours before anyone would come for them, and Mat was right; it was far too cold, even in their heavy clothes, to wait here for seven hours — until way after midnight, possibly longer. Surely the fog would lift soon. But even if it did, night was almost here and it would be dark. Were there houses anywhere near? He tried to remember.

Meg was thinking along with him, and Mat, too. Meg said, "I remember seeing a cottage near the road. It was a long way back."

"There was a tent after that," Mat said. "But it was a long way back, too."

Suddenly, without seeing it, Tim stumbled into the face of a rock looming up in the fog. He put his hand out and ran it over the surface. It went on around to the left, and it was big. If they could get to the other side, it would shelter them from the wind, and then they could sit down and wait. He said, "Be careful, the ground is uneven. We'll edge around the left."

It was hard going. The earth beneath them, the rocks, sloped steeply down. They half slid, half walked down and then around the rock. Tim got his flashlight from its loop on his belt again, and turned it toward the rock. There was a crevice in the rock, not very wide, only about two feet. But maybe it was hollow. He stepped forward cautiously and moved into the crevice with Meg following, holding on to Mat. They were all inside the crevice, and the wind could not touch them. There seemed to be more room ahead, inside the rock. Tim moved forward, using the flashlight, and they really were inside the rock, protected from all sides. The floor flattened out, and the fog was not nearly so thick. As Tim turned the light downward to the floor, he felt a twinge of excitement. There was a flat place for four or five feet and then what looked like wide, crude steps, leading down.

Meg said, "Are those *steps?*"

Mat said slowly, "I bet we've come to the sea. I bet this is a way down to the sea."

They stood still and listened. Was there a sound of water far below? The sound of waves breaking on the shore? Were they really near the sea? The pond where they had been fishing was not far from the sea, from St. Mary's Bay, they knew that. But steps? Leading down to the shore? It didn't make sense. Except that in Newfoundland, so old, it might make sense. One of the things Dick Ackley had told them, days ago, was that people were not supposed to have started building houses in Newfoundland until about a hundred and fifty years ago. Just today, Hugh Crocker had said that the Devon fishermen didn't want settlements. What if somebody had built a house up here, out of sight of the sea, and finding this break in the rock, had carved out steps to make it easier to get down to fish?

"Let's try it," Mat said. "What have we got to lose? Maybe there's an Outport at the foot of these steps, Tim. There might be. Houses, and people . . . even a *little* Outport would be wonderful. We're pretty sure to get kind of hungry after a while."

Tim went forward slowly, flashing the light downward. The fog was shut out. The rock was damp, the steps were damp, but they were broad and easy. But there were only five of them, and then a long, long passageway, a tunnel, really, showed up ahead.

Meg stopped. "I don't like this very much," she said. "I really don't, Tim. How do we know what we're getting

65

into? Maybe ... all of a sudden ... we'll come to the edge ... and the sea below. .... I don't like it. I think we'd better go back."

"What's the use of going back?" Mat said. "It can't take too long to find out where this tunnel goes. Tim, have you got a new battery in that flashlight?"

"Yes, and two more in my pocket," Tim said. "It won't hurt to have a look, Meg. Mat's right. There must be something along here, or why the steps? There could be an Outport. They build them everywhere on the shore."

Meg didn't answer, but she followed along. The tunnel was straight; it was about three feet wide and looked sometimes like an ordinary split in the rock and sometimes as if it had been hollowed out a little here and there. After a while it turned and began to slope down again, and there were more steps.

And then, suddenly, the tunnel came to an end. Before them was another crevice in the rock, very narrow. Tim stood staring at it.

Mat said in a calm voice, "I keep thinking about pirate ghosts. I keep thinking about that old pirate, Sir Henry, climbing up to meet us with a cutlass in his teeth."

"Be quiet," Meg said. "I'm scared enough already. Let's go back, Tim. We shouldn't have come down here. They might be looking for us up near the road, and they'd never find us. Never."

"If they've come back to look for us, they'll keep looking," Tim heard himself saying. "You know that. I want to know what's on the other side of that crack in the rock."

"So do I," Mat said. "I sure do, lad."

Tim moved into the crevice. It was almost too narrow to

get through, and it turned and twisted every couple of feet. Meg and Mat were close behind him.

Then, suddenly, he heard the lapping of water; not the rush of the waves, but the slow gentle lapping of water in a quiet place. He took two more steps and found himself out in the open, right out in a big open place, or it felt open. There was a large stone about two feet in front of the narrow crevice, but the place felt open. He stepped out, turned and walked two yards, and he was past the stone. Now he was looking at fog, seeping in through a faraway opening in the rock, and at the sea, lapping the shore right below.

But they were not out in the open.

Mat said, "Listen! Listen, Tim."

His voice came back again and again. Listen, listen, listen.

"It's a cave," Mat said. "It's a great big cave."

Tim turned the flashlight up and around and down. It certainly was a cave, a very big cave, with a stone roof and stone walls. It was open to the ocean, low down, anyway; the water lay here, sea water.

But it was when he turned the flashlight back on the crevice, toward the way from which they had come, that they got their big surprise. The stone wall blocking the entrance to the crevice was the back of a fireplace, the biggest fireplace anybody had ever seen. It really was a fireplace, and people had cooked in it. There was a black iron kettle hanging from a crane, a cooking kettle. It looked at least a hundred years old.

CHAPTER
7

AFTER A LONG MINUTE, while they all stared at the fireplace and the kettle and the disintegrated small boat lying on the sand above the water's edge; at the vastness and eeriness of the cave and the water lapping gently on the sloping sandy floor of the cave, Mat said in a calm voice, "The question is, is the tide in or out?"

Tim and Meg both looked at him and at each other. Tim took a long breath. He felt as if he were living in a dream, but he wasn't. He was here, they were all here, in a big old cave, a secret-looking cave, somewhere on the shore of Newfoundland. It was true.

"The tide?" he heard himself saying. "Well, it's in. It's going out. You can see the high-water mark about six inches up from the water. So it's going out."

"Well, that's something," Mat decided. "We don't have to

go back up into the tunnel." He was doing something with his fishing rod. Suddenly, he flung the line into the water, and as if all this were magic, the line tightened instantly. Mat jerked forward and then stiffened himself, and then he reeled in a fish, a big one, fifteen inches long anyway. It didn't make any trouble. Mat just reeled it in, and there it hung, from the end of the rod. Tim reached up with a dazed feeling and took it off the hook. "I thought so," Mat said, in a satisfied way. "I guess we're in business, Tim. Have you got matches?"

"Of course I've got matches."

Meg took off her red knitted gloves and laid them on the ledge at the end of the ancient fireplace. She said, "The wood from that old boat will burn. We can have a fire. I can cook the fish in sea water in that old kettle. We can skin it afterwards, so if the kettle's dirty it won't matter. If we have a nice bright fire and something to eat we'll all feel better. Tim, you clean the fish with your Scout knife. Mat, you and I can get the wood."

Still feeling dazed, Tim got his sharp knife from its leather sheath. He laid the fish down on the clean sand, cut off its head and slit it open. He kept expecting to wake up any minute and find that they were up on the marsh, lost, cold, wandering in the terrible fog.

Meg and Mat came with armloads of wood. They dropped it down in front of the fireplace so that Tim could lay the fire. His fires always worked. He got down on his knees and stacked the wood together properly, small bits first, underneath the kettle. It was a very heavy kettle, but he managed to lift it off its hook and carry it down to the water to rinse it out, and then get some clean sea water in

70

it. He took it back and hung it from the crane. He got his matches from their waterproof case in his pocket and took one from the.box. He said to Meg, "Have you got some paper handkerchiefs? Then I won't have to whittle shavings, maybe."

She unwound her red knitted scarf and unbuttoned her jacket. She gave him three paper handkerchiefs from an inside pocket. He knelt down, stuffed the paper under the slivered wood and started to strike the match on the box. At that very second he heard Mat say "Shhh!" and he did not strike the match. He got up.

Mat was pointing to the low archway at the front of the cave, the archway that led to the sea. It was much lighter outside than when they had come into the cave; the fog seemed to be lifting. Against the light, they could see something moving. It was a boat with a man in it. It came silently, silently, under the arch, the oars dipping softly, secretively.

The three of them moved without thinking; they got back quickly behind the heavy wall of the fireplace. Afterwards, none of them could explain why each one had felt they had to hide. A man rowing a boat? He could rescue them. He could take them out of this strange place; he could take them to safety. But it was because the place was so strange, so silent, so secret and because the boat moved so stealthily that they felt stealthy too.

The boat came on into the cave, but not far. It stopped on the opposite side, against the rock wall. The man stepped out of the boat and tied it to something fixed into the rock, probably a big iron ring. He was dressed in oilskins; high rubber boots, a long black oilskin coat, an oilskin fisherman's hat pulled down on his head. They could scarcely see him at all; it was only the archway of vague light that showed him when he moved against it. But as soon as he had tied the boat, he took a strong flashlight from his pocket and turned its beam against the wall. As he pressed the button the beam turned for an instant toward the fireplace, and the children ducked. But he was not interested in that end of the cave. He reached up, found another ring in the rock and pulled himself up to a ledge climbing the side of the cave. He walked up the ledge four or five paces, and then the light showed that he had turned into a crevice in the rock, a crevice such as the one they had come by. He was gone for a long time.

Mat stirred. He opened his mouth. Tim clamped his hand over it. But Meg whispered in his ear, "He's a man, Tim! Why can't we ask him for help?"

Tim shook his head. "Wait," he said. "Be quiet!"

The light shone out of the crevice, and the man appeared again. He was carrying something — a bag. Making his way carefully down the ledge, he dropped the bag into the boat. He went up again, vanished into the crevice and came out with another bag. He did the same thing four times. Then, at last, he untied the boat and got into it. Meg pulled frantically at Tim's arm, but he just shook his head.

The boat was gone.

They were all very quiet, waiting. The faint sound of the oars died away.

Tim said, "We've got rubber boots on. We can wade to that ledge. What's up in that place he went to?"

Meg said, "Oh, no, Tim! Don't think about pirate treasure! You know what it must be? Rum, or something like that.

72

People smuggle things in to Newfoundland, don't they? They smuggle things everywhere. That's what is up there, I know it. Some foreign boat anchors offshore and men bring rum ashore and hide it here and then that man comes and gets it and sells it. That's all it will be, you'll see."

"So what? We've got to know, anyway."

"Me," Mat said gravely, "I wouldn't rest easy if I didn't know. Maybe there isn't any left, whatever he came after. But maybe there'll be something to show what it was."

"He might come back," Meg said. "If this is smuggling, he wouldn't like it a bit if we were spying on him!"

Tim walked into the water, out toward the archway. It was shallow. The tide was going out fast. He went on walking until he was within fifteen feet of the archway, and the water was only up to his knees. He turned. "He can't come back," he said. "By now there isn't enough water to float his boat." He spoke as quietly as he could, but his voice almost boomed in the enormous empty cavern.

Mat waded in too, and then finally Meg followed. They made their way across to the ring in the rock wall. The one the man had pulled himself up by was far too high for them to reach, but there were two others lower down.

"Big," Mat said. "I think those rings were elephant bracelets, one time. Maybe."

They were old and rusty. Tim pulled carefully on the lowest one, but it held firm. He got himself up to the ledge that sloped right away down under water. He started to move up carefully. The rock slope was wet where the man had walked in his dripping boots. Mat was right behind Tim, and Meg followed, watching over her shoulder. There wasn't any danger. The water was almost all gone; they would be able to crawl under that arch on the sand in just a few minutes. The man couldn't come back . . . unless . . . well, unless . . .

"Hurry up," Mat said. "Maybe he doesn't always bring the boat in. Maybe he'll come walking back."

Tim got to the opening of the crevice. He turned on the flashlight, and all he could see was a narrow slit in the rock. But this wasn't the beginning of a passageway. When he stepped inside, he turned one corner and he was facing a blank wall. There was no opening, no passageway, nothing but a blank wall.

Mat came to stand beside him, and then Meg. Tim flashed his light over the rock in front and was baffled. The man had taken four bags of something from here; had they been piled here on the floor, in this small space, in the very opening of the crevice? Where else? Yet it had looked as if he had gone farther into the crevice. His flashlight had vanished, hadn't it?

"Nothing," Meg said hopefully.

"Not a thing," Tim said. "Nothing at all."

"Well, jeepers," Mat said sadly. "There ought to be *something*."

"There isn't," Tim said, and turned. "Go on down, you two. These bags must have been piled up here in this little spot where we're standing. That's all. There's nothing else here."

As he spoke, he put out his hand to steady himself in turning. The heavy grey rock wall, seamed and streaked exactly like all the rest of the cavern wall, moved under his hand. It moved. Startled, he turned his flashlight on it and pushed. It moved again.

74

He said slowly, "Kids, it's canvas. Hold everything."

He slid a hand along and found the edge of the heavy stuff. He pushed with his shoulder. It was a grey curtain, weighted down with rocks, painted to look like stone. But it moved aside easily. He flashed his torch on ahead, and there was a little room behind the canvas, a room carved out by tools, a square room with a low ceiling. He went in, and Mat and Meg followed him. The canvas fell into place behind them.

It was a neat little room. It was piled with boxes, metal boxes, old and heavy, with raised patterns on the lids and sides. The top box in the left-hand pile was locked with an old-fashioned hasp and padlock. But the box on the right was not locked Tim reached down and opened the lid. The box was half full of what looked like bars of lead. He picked one up, and it was a lot heavier than he expected. He turned it over and over in his hand, then put it back into the box. "Lead," he said. "Why would they drag heavy boxes of lead up here?"

Mat had pushed past him and was bending over a leather bag lying on the floor. The neck was tied shut with a leather lace, but it was very old; when Mat pulled at it, the lace broke. The leather was very stiff, but it came open. They could see what was inside.

After a long time Meg said, "The luck of the Pattersons. That's all I've got to say."

Tim stared into the bag. He said, "We'd better get out of here. That's all *I've* got to say. This is much too big for a bunch of kids to fool around with. We just better get out of here fast."

"Not without samples," Mat said softly. He reached into

the bag, took out two round gold coins and put them into his pocket. "Nobody would believe us without samples." He reached in again and handed two more coins to Tim. His hand went into the bag once more to fumble in the contents. He brought out something small and shiny and handed it to Meg. She took it without looking at it, still staring into that leather bag. She pushed it into her pocket.

"Try to shut the bag again," Tim heard himself saying. He held the light. Mat squeezed the old leather back into place. Tim lifted the lid of the unlocked box again and took up one of the heavy bars. He got out his knife and scratched the bar. Under the blade the metal beneath the old greyness gleamed suddenly bright. Tim rubbed the scratch with his thumb so that it almost disappeared.

They left the little room and went back down the slope. They didn't even think of turning again toward the fireplace, with the fire laid ready to light and the freshly caught fish. Without saying anything to one another, they went to the archway under the stone. The tide had gone out six feet or more beyond the arch, and the sand was bare. The arch was higher than it looked; Mat could walk under it almost upright, and Meg and Tim didn't have to bend very much. In a minute or two they were out in the open air on the seashore. The fog was lifting, and it was still daylight. Tim looked at his watch and was shocked; it was only half-past six. It was only an hour and a half since the cars had left for St. John's.

CHAPTER

8

THERE HAD BEEN no fog in St. John's. But by half-past eight
Mrs. Patterson was beginning to worry about the children;
they should be home. They had been gone since eleven in
the morning She knew it was a long way to St. Mary's Bay,
but surely not so far that it would take all this time to come
home. Emmy and Dierdre Merrick were only babies, nine
and ten, and Tom Merrick wouldn't keep them out on the
cold marshes fishing for too many hours. She waited at the
hotel; finally she telephoned Mollie Crocker.

"Oh, Lucy darlin', don't be worryin'," Mollie said. "Hughie
wouldn't let a thing go wrong, and you know it. They get
throwin' the lines in, thim men, and they forget all about
time. Likely they'll come home with a long string of nice

trout. Maybe your boys are as bad as ours — they don't know whin to stop, if the trout start bitin'."

Lucy Patterson put down the phone and tried not to worry, but the hands of the clock went on and on; soon it was nine o'clock, and no children yet. But at a quarter after nine Janet Kennedy telephoned. She said, "Pat's home, Lucy, with Jerry and Moira, and Ricky Crocker. And Tom Merrick's along, too, with Emmy and Dierdre. Your three are with Hughie Crocker — they wanted to stay together, the children say. The fog came down and they had a bit of a scramble to get to the cars, but it's all right. They've all squashed into Hughie's car; Gilly Merrick, and your three, and Paul and Jamie Crocker. They'll be along any minute now."

But they weren't. Hughie Crocker's car was limping along the highway, stopping every fifteen minutes because the engine was overheating. The fog had lifted, and as the car finally came into the last stretch, the lights of St. John's were brilliant in the distance. The children were hungry. Hugh dropped Gilly Merrick off at the Merrick house and went on home.

It was after ten o'clock when he knocked on Lucy Patterson's door at the hotel. She opened it to find him standing there white-faced. He was alone. She stared at him. He came into the room and shut the door. He glanced round the room quickly, hopefully, and then took off his glasses and put a hand over his eyes.

"Hughie?"

He said huskily, "You've not heard from the children?"

"My children? Hughie! How could I have heard from them?"

He shook his head. "There must have been other cars on

79

the road. That's all I keep saying to myself. Surely there would have been other cars on the road."

Lucy Patterson sat down slowly on the edge of the sofa. "Tell me," she said gently.

"It's my fault. I should have counted. I thought I had. We all thought we had. Meg and Tim got into Tom Merrick's car. He shut the door after them, he knows they got into his car. They must have got right out again, looking for Mat. The children, our children, say that your three talked about having to be together. . . ."

"Yes. I made them promise. Yes."

"So the two bigger ones must have gone looking for Mat."

"And they weren't in any of the cars? You mean . . . they didn't come home with anybody? Meg and Tim and Mat? They aren't here, Hugh?"

"They're not here," he said steadily. "I came . . . I thought maybe somebody else had picked them up. Maybe somebody has, Lucy. They were right at the road. They wouldn't have left it. They're bright. And other people are driving that road, now in the summer. . . ." He went to the telephone. "Get me the highway police," he told the operator.

Lucy sat waiting, her hands locked together in her lap, her mind blank. If somebody else had picked up the children, they would have come straight here. They would know that she would worry until she heard from them. They were very responsible children.

She heard Hugh talking to the police; she knew by his questions and replies that there was no report. She couldn't sit and wait. She opened the door, ran out into the hall, pressed the elevator button and went down to the lobby. She looked frantically around, hoping — but knowing it was

80

foolish to hope — that the children were there. They were not there. The Manrens were in the lobby; they had been out of the city all day. Lucy said, "Oh, do excuse me, but my children haven't come home — did you see them or hear of them anywhere?"

Mrs. Manred said in her little-girl voice, "Didn't come home? The children? Should we have seen them? Where were they?"

"They went fishing with their cousins," Lucy said steadily. "But somehow — they got separated. Maybe someone else picked them up along the road."

"Along what road?" Mr. Manren said carefully. "Where were they, Mrs. Patterson?"

"I don't know exactly. Somewhere out toward St. Mary's Bay. They went to a pond away out there . . . and the fog came . . ." she stopped.

Someone was whistling nearby. Dick Ackley came in. He had a raincoat over his arm, and his hair looked wet. He looked at Lucy and stopped whistling. His eyes went to the Manrens and back to her. "Something wrong?" he asked.

It was Mr. Manren who answered. "The Patterson children seem to be missing," he said. "They went fishing with some cousins and they haven't come back."

"Where?"

Lucy said, trying to keep her voice steady, "Somewhere out toward St. Mary's Bay. Crewes' Pond. Out on . . . on the marshes. It's . . . away up there on the marshes . . . people can get . . . I mean, in the fog . . ."

"They got left behind?" Dick Ackley asked sharply.

"There were three cars. A lot of children. People got mixed up. Everybody thought my children were with somebody else. But they were down at the road. Were you out that way, Mr. Ackley? Can you think of anything? We're trying the highway police, but —"

He didn't answer. His eyes were dark, thoughtful.

Mr. Manren said slowly, "The highway police?"

"My cousin is talking to them. Surely somebody must have picked up the children. They wouldn't go off the road. They are very responsible children. And Tim has a lot of Scout training — he took his compass and . . . he has a flashlight . . ." She remembered Tim saying, "Shall I take my hatchet, Mom, in case we get nailed up in a cask?" She put her hands suddenly over her face.

Hughie Crocker came out of the elevator. He walked rapidly across the lobby and said, "We're getting a dozen men together, Lucy. We'll go right back. If nobody picked them up, they'll be waiting there. Tim's got a lot of sense. He knows that when you get lost you sit still and wait. But . . . we'll take men to cover the whole area. The fog has lifted out there now, the police say. We'll find them, Lucy."

"I'll go," Mr. Manren said. "Exactly where?"

Dick Ackley said quickly, "How far out toward St. Mary's?"

"Just beyond Little Deer Road," Hugh said. "But you're not islanders. We can do with all the help there is, but when you don't know the country you can't help, for all we're grateful for the offer."

"Little Deer Road," Mr. Manren repeated. "Is that out beyond Father Duffy's Well? I know the Well."

"It's maybe forty miles beyond. We went to Crewes' Pond." He settled his coat. "The police are coming in from the other way, Lucy. We might get a report from them any minute. But we'll not wait."

82

Mrs. Manren said, "Oh, surely there are houses out there? Surely people live nearby? Surely what's happened is that the children have got to some house where the people haven't a car or a telephone . . . and the police will check, won't they? They'll check every house?" She looked up at her husband. "You wouldn't be much use, Randle. You wouldn't be any use at all — you don't know the island. There'll be lots of cars on the road."

"You're probably quite right," he said, "I'd just be another problem."

From the hotel desk, a voice spoke loudly. "Mrs. Patterson? We have a telephone call for you."

Lucy turned. She said blankly, "A telephone call?" It would be Molly, or Janet Kennedy or Ellen Merrick. The desk clerk held out the receiver. She took it. "Hello?"

Tim's voice spoke. Tim. He said, "Mom? You worrying about us? We're fine. We're all fine. We're lucky. There's a telephone here."

She couldn't speak. After a minute she made a sound of some kind, and he said again, quickly, "Mom! We're fine. Did the others get home all right in the fog? We're coming to St. Joseph's in a motorboat. Can you get somebody with a car to meet us there?"

She couldn't speak. She turned to Hugh Crocker who was beside her. He took the telephone. "Who is it?" he said. "Who are you?"

He listened. As he listened, he put an arm around Lucy's shoulders. She began to get collected. Hugh said, "That's wonderful, Tim. It's wonderful. Only how in the name of heaven did you get to Charity's Garden? How did you get there?"

He listened again. "All right, I've got it," he said. "Mr.

Potter will take you up to St. Joseph's. We'll meet you there. You'd better speak to your mother again, and let Meg and Mat speak too. She's had a shock, boy."

Lucy took the telephone. Tim said eagerly, "Mom, some fishermen picked us up and brought us here to this Outport, Charity's Garden, and we've had a swell supper, pork and potatoes and greens, and Mr. Potter, the storekeeper, is warming up his motorboat and he's going to take us up to St. Joseph's, up the Bay. Mom? You all right?"

"I am now," Lucy said. "And Meg? And Mat?"

They came and spoke to her. Mat was last. Just before he hung up, he said in his small quiet voice, "We had a real adventure, Mom. You better be prepared."

She turned from the telephone. They were all looking at her, Hugh Crocker and Mr. and Mrs. Manren and Dick Ackley. She said, half laughing and half crying, "I don't know why I worry about those three. They get out of everything. Mat says they've had a real adventure. I can't even imagine what."

"Good kids," Dick Ackley said evenly. "They're good kids."

But Hugh Crocker was frowning. "I don't get it at all. How on earth did they get to Charity's Garden? It's only about five houses — away out on the tip of Bagley's Point. Tim says some fishermen picked them up, so they must have got down to the sea. But that's on the other side of the road. We were troutin' on the north side, and they'd have had to cross the road and get across an impossible stretch of marshland to get down to the shore. It can't be done. I don't understand. If they'd got their feet on the road, they'd have stayed on it. Tim's got sense about things like that. He wouldn't have let them all wander into the marshes. There's nothing but marsh on the south side, all the way down to the shore."

"The road isn't smooth around there," Dick Ackley said. "They might have crossed it in the fog without realizing they were on it. They must have."

"But how did they get across the marshes? It's impossible."

Mr. Manren ran a hand over his bald head. He said evenly, "Children can often accomplish the impossible."

CHAPTER
9

When Mr. Potter's motorboat slid into the wharf at St. Joseph's, the three grown cousins were waiting for the children: Hugh Crocker, Pat Kennedy and Tom Merrick. It was late; it was way past midnight, and Meg and Tim and Mat all knew that they should be sleepy and tired, half dead, maybe. But they weren't. They were far too excited.

They had made up their minds what had to be done. When they were building the bonfire on the shore, far south of the entrance to the cave, they had made a firm compact not to let the smallest hint drop of what they had found. It was too big to talk about, it was far too big. It had been easy to keep quiet about it at the Outport. All they had to do was act stupid, keep saying that they were mainlanders and didn't know where they had been or how they had got where they were. They didn't know, exactly, so that wasn't much of a lie. The fishermen who picked them up had been curious, though. They had been kind, and they had been anxious to get the children to shore and back to their mother as soon as possible. How the children ever got to the ocean was beyond them; the cliffs were high and straight, and there were marshes above; it seemed as if nobody had ever come to that strip of shore except by boat. Their own Outport, Charity's Garden, was across a narrow inlet. It hadn't taken very long to get across to it, and meanwhile all three of them, Meg and Tim and Mat, acted as if they were tired out and hadn't a clue about anything. Mr. Potter had asked a few sharp questions, but it wasn't any use. Mainland children just didn't know anything about Newfoundland, they couldn't tell north from south, they had probably been troutin' somewhere away south of the road. It didn't matter.

Mr. Potter wouldn't take any pay for bringing them home. He laughed when Hugh Crocker brought the subject up.

"Don't be daft, man," he said. "It's only a step here an' back. I've got youngun's o' me own." And he had gunned his motor and raced away, back to Charity's Garden and his old rickety store perched on the rock, looking as if it were about ready to topple into the ocean.

They got to the hotel finally. All three cousins went upstairs with the children. They were very quiet, very unhappy men. They blamed themselves. But it hadn't been their fault; Meg and Tim tried to make that clear when they were safe inside their own sitting room in the hotel, with the door shut and no strangers around. "We *did* get into your car, Tom," Meg said. "Tim and I both got in and we knew you thought we were there. But we got out to look for Mat. And you didn't know about Mat falling down, Pat, because he fell on his face and he couldn't make a sound until you'd gone right past him. He wasn't on the path, he fell a yard away from it. It's all right."

"It could have been desprit," said Pat. He looked as if he had been in a torture chamber. "All I can say is, thanks to the Blessed Virgin, ye're safe. There's been a lot of prayers said for you three, this night. A great lot of prayers."

It was Tom Merrick who said slowly, lighting his pipe, "It's not at all clear, Tim, how you got down to the shore across from Charity's Garden. You all seemed so sleepy in the car, we asked no questions. But it's a big mystery. It can't be done. And why did you cross the road in the first place? Why not stay on it, when you found it? It's not criticizing I'm doing," he said hastily. "It's just asking. I'd have been sure you'd have stayed on the road."

"We didn't cross the road," Tim said.

"But you had to, boy. Crewes' Pond, where we were troutin', is on the north side of the road. Nobody ever tries to get to any of the ponds on the south, because that marsh is treacherous. There isn't a safe path over it anywhere. But Potter says the fishermen picked you up somewhere across from Charity. That is away down shore from the road . . . away south. And the cliffs just there are straight, some places a couple of hundred feet high. Even if you could get to them, you couldn't get down to shore. It's never been done. And how did you get to them?"

Tim and Meg and Mat looked at one another. Tim's eyes rested on Hugh Crocker's steady face, his clear wise eyes behind the glasses. He took a long breath. He said slowly, "Well, we did have an adventure. It's pretty big. It's so big

89

it scares us. We have to tell you. It isn't anything for kids to get mixed up with, we've got enough sense to know that." He glanced at the others again and put his hand into his pocket. He brought out the two gold coins, rosy and heavy, and put them carefully on the table. Mat took his hand from his mother's and came to lay his coins beside them. And Meg went into the bedroom and came out with her jacket; she slipped her hand into the pocket and took out the lovely thing that was there. She put it on the table. It glittered and sparkled in the light.

The three men had all stood up. They were standing and staring down at the table. After a long time Pat Kennedy put out his hand and touched the little figurine Meg had laid down. It was about five inches high, a woman, made of gold; she stood on a field of emeralds, holding a baby. Around her head was a crown of stars — a crown of diamonds.

"Holy Mary," said Pat reverently. "It's de Blessed Virgin herself. It's de Blessed Virgin herself."

It took a long time then to explain what had happened; where they had been, what they had seen, what they had found. The men couldn't grasp it. There was something wrong about the geography, even when they could realize that there was an enormous cave fronting on the sea and hidden in the cave this unbelievable horde of treasure. It was as if all the lost legends had suddenly come to life, and yet the coming to life wasn't real.

Tom Merrick said, "When they were inching along the rock, they must have been inching along the road itself. This must be so. And they came to the top of the cliffs, not knowing — and the pile of rock is there, on the north of the

road. Right beside the road. The entrance to the passage-way."

"Niver mind that," Pat said nervously. "What's to be done now, boy? Who is this man, knowin' the cave and the treasure, takin' it away? Who is he?" He looked from Meg to Tim and Mat. "Ye had no glimpse of his face, ye can't say who he might have been?"

"It was dark," Tim said. "There wasn't any light except what came under the archway, and the fog was still heavy. He turned on his torch, but he didn't ever turn it on his face, not for a second. All we know is that he was tall. He could have been fat or he could have been thin, because he was dressed in a heavy oilskin coat and a big sou'wester hat pulled right down. And big boots. He could have been anybody, and we wouldn't know him anyway, would we?"

"It is an islander he's got to be," Pat Kennedy said. "But where did he come from? Where did he row his boat to, wid his new load? What kind of an islander is he, then, to keep so mum? How long has he known about this, and how much has he taken away, and what's he managed to do wid it? He's a smart lad, whoever he is, and that's to be sure. But who is he?"

"Whoever he is," Hugh Crocker said very quietly, "he wouldn't like being found out. He wouldn't like it at all." He sat down. "This is a bad business."

"A bad business?" Pat echoed. "Man, where's your wits? A bad business, with all Newfoundland's needin'?" He turned to Tim anxiously. "Ye know the way back, lad? Ye know?"

Meg said carefully, "We marked it."

"You marked it?"

Meg said, "Tim, you tell it."

Tim thought things over. He said, "Well, it was like this. The minute we got out of the cave and looked back, we could see that nobody would ever guess there was a cave there. It's away back in an inlet, with a long arm of land stretching out on either side. And right in front of the entrance it looks as if some time or another there's been a big rock fall, a real big rock fall, and there's just a tremendous big pile of rocks lying there. It would take smart steering to get a boat in, and nobody would try if he didn't know where he was going." He stopped. "The rocks are on the right-hand side of the cave, that's north. I started using my compass when we left the cave. It didn't do any good before that because I didn't know what to start from."

"You climbed over the rocks?"

"No, nobody could do that. They're too big. Part of the cliff. We had to go the other way. At first we started to walk out to the end of that point, but we couldn't make it. No path, too many rocks, and no shore — so we climbed over that point. And Meg got the idea that maybe we could never find the place again."

Meg said, "Mom, it was my new red scarf, the one we bought at Nonia's to match the red gloves. You know. It was hand-knitted. I hated to do it, but I unravelled it and broke little bits of red wool off, and we kept tying them to branches as we climbed over the rocks. When we got over that first piece of land, we came to a long stretch of shore, and at first we thought we'd build a signal fire there . . ."

"But the guy might come back," Mat broke in. "We didn't know where he was. We were too close."

Tom Merrick looked up quickly and back again at his pipe. He said nothing.

"So," Tim continued, "we didn't build a fire there. We

93

were tired, but we thought we better keep on going. We climbed over about six points of land and went along a lot of little bays, and then we thought we were far enough away, and we built a bonfire. The fog was nearly gone, and we hoped maybe some fishermen would be out early or somebody would see the fire from somewhere — and they did. We weren't there half an hour before four men rowed in near enough so we could yell for help. And they took us over to Charity's Garden."

"And you tied this red wool all the way from the cave to the place where you built the bonfire?" Hughie Crocker asked.

"Yes, we did. Not too close together. But we can follow it back."

His mother said anxiously, "Tim, this man — are you sure he didn't see you?"

"He couldn't have seen us. We didn't make a sound in the cave. We were hiding behind the fireplace. And when we crawled out of the archway, we were careful. We looked for the boat, but it was out of sight. We don't know which way he went. But he was gone, and we never saw a hint of him again."

There was a long silence. Hughie Crocker got up and started walking up and down the floor.

"I guess something has to be done," Tim said.

Tom Merrick took his pipe out of his mouth. He looked at Hugh. He said, "Maybe it should go right to Joey himself."

Hugh didn't answer. Mat said, "Who is this Joey everybody talks about? Who is he?"

Pat Kennedy said incredulously, "Joey? You don't know about Joey?"

Tom Merrick said gently, "He's our prime minister. He does a lot for the country."

Hugh said, "It can't go right to Joey. We'd have to explain our business to somebody else in order to get to Joey."

"Well then?"

"There's only one man," Hugh said. He went to the telephone, asked for a number. He said, when somebody answered, "Sir, it's important. Could you come to Room 416 at the Newfoundland Hotel? This is Hugh Crocker. It's an urgent matter."

He didn't say a name. He didn't explain anything. Everybody in the room was sitting still, thinking. Tim began to feel so sleepy that he wondered how much longer he could stay awake. He was ashamed of himself, but it was true. Meg was sitting with her head back against her chair. But not Mat. His eyes were as bright as the jewels in the crown of the Blessed Virgin lying on the table.

Hugh Crocker took a newspaper casually from the table beside the sofa. He laid it over the coins and the little figurine.

There was a knock at the door. Hugh went to open it. The man standing there was middle-aged, steady-looking, heavy. His eyes went over everyone in the room in half a second. He shut the door.

"This is Inspector Fitzgerald, of the Mounted Police," Hugh Crocker said. "Inspector, these young people have something to tell you."

*　 *　 *

Fifteen minutes later, Inspector Fitzgerald stood at the table, looking again and again at the four gold coins and the little statuette. He had asked questions, very clear and careful questions. When he got an answer, he had a way of

95

nodding — not saying anything, but adding it up in his mind.

At last he said, "You're quite certain, now, Tim, and you, Meg, and you, Mat, that you didn't peep a word to the four fishermen, or anyone at the Outport — Mrs. Potter, who gave you your supper, for instance — or Mr. Potter, that would let them guess you were excited, that you had found the cave and what was in it? That you had found *anything?*"

"I know we didn't," Tim said. "We — you see, our father is a geologist. He's always finding gold or silver or uranium or oil or something. That's his job. And ever since we could talk, we've heard him saying that you mustn't ever say a word about anything you've found that's specially valuable. You have to wait until you can tell the right people. Because if you tell the wrong people, bad things can happen, very bad things."

"I see." The inspector's eyes went over all three of them again, measuring them. He looked at their mother, and his firm mouth curved into a faint smile. "You're to be congratulated, Mrs. Patterson," he said.

"Thank you. And Inspector, it's so terribly late — do you think they might go to bed? They are a great deal more exhausted than they realize."

"I'm sure of that. Can you give me just a few more minutes?"

She didn't answer. He didn't wait for an answer. He turned and picked up the telephone from the desk. "Room 206, please," he said. And in a minute, "Will you come up to 416, sir?"

Hugh Crocker and Pat and Tom all looked at him in surprise. He was the head of the Mounted Police in New-

foundland. Who would he call "sir"? The prime minister?
But the prime minister didn't live in the hotel. And even
the head of the Mounted Police wouldn't call the prime
minister at three o'clock in the morning without any prepa-
ration, would he?

It was a few minutes before the knock came at the door.
The inspector opened it. The man outside was Mr. Lewis
Jones, not looking as if he had just got out of bed; his
tie was tied, his jacket buttoned, his hair neat. There was a
faint stubble on his chin, nothing more to show that he
hadn't been dressed and waiting. He gave the inspector
a long inquiring glance and came in. Inspector Fitzgerald
said, "You've likely not met Mr. Jones, Mrs. Patterson and
gentlemen. He keeps to himself. You'll need to know that
Mr. Jones is not exactly Mr. Jones. He has another name
and an official title in Ottawa. He came to Newfoundland
on a special mission, and it looks as if these children may
have found an answer for him." To Mr. Jones he indicated
the three men, who stood waiting. He gave their names.
Then he went to the table, and with a kind of flourish, the
first sign of excitement that he had shown, he lifted the
newspaper covering the coins and the statuette. He didn't
say anything.

Mr. Jones moved forward. It was as if the things on the
table were strong magnets. He stared at them. He picked
up a coin, turned it over in his hand, took an odd glass
from his breast pocket and looked at the coin carefully. He
said absently, "Seventeen fifty-three." He put it down,
took up each of the others. Finally he lifted the statuette.
He turned it over and over, front and back, and looked at
each of the jewels in the crown and in the emerald grass.

97

He laid it down. He took a long breath. "Where?" he asked.

"Here. In a cave somewhere on the shore of St. Mary's Bay. The children came upon it by accident, but they have marked its whereabouts and they can find it again."

"Does anyone else know?"

"No one except the people in this room."

Mr. Jones' eyes were not steel grey now. They were blue, but the pale blue of the coldest winter ice. They rested on Hugh Crocker's face and on Tom Merrick's and on Pat Kennedy's. They came back to the inspector, who nodded without speaking.

Mr. Jones said slowly, "We have been looking for something like this for a long time. Are these pieces all that remained in the cave?"

Tim took a long breath. "There are boxes and boxes still in the cave. We only opened two. One had a lot of those gold coins in it. There was a leather bag with gems, things like the statuette and crowns and rings and loose stones. But the other box was more than half full of bars of metal. They looked like lead, but when I scratched one with my knife, I could see it was gold."

It was Mat who spoke in a sleepy voice. He said, "We're not the only ones who know, Inspector."

Inspector Fitzgerald looked at him, startled. Then he smiled. "Of course, Mat. What I am saying, sir, is that nobody but the people in this room know anything about the children's discovery. There is a man who is taking it away. The children saw him but they don't know him."

Mr. Jones said carefully, "I'm sure you'll give me the full story, Inspector. We'll have to take immediate action. I must stress with everything in my power that all of you here, every one of you here, must not allow one word or hint or inflection of voice to show that you know anything about this. This is desperately important."

Pat Kennedy straightened. "I give ye my word, sir, for one. My wife, she's a wan for ferritin' out bits o' news, but I'll be like the grave."

Hughie Crocker said steadily, "I don't think we underestimate the problem, Mr. Jones. I think we understand."

Tom Merrick shook his head. "I'd think the best thing that could happen would be for the Patterson children to leave Newfoundland right away, sir. They won't talk, I know we can trust them, but how do we know what that man might guess or figure out? There's been a bit of a to-do in the hotel tonight about the children being lost — and out near St. Mary's Bay. There are things we don't know about this story. Suppose the man the inspector will tell you of, sir, saw these children after all? Suppose he did?"

Mr. Jones stood without speaking or moving. Then he said, "It's time they were in bed now. I think, Inspector Fitzgerald, that you and I must excuse ourselves and retire to hold a council of war."

CHAPTER

10

THE NEXT DAY, Tim and Hughie Crocker were in a rented
motor launch, making a trip from St. Joseph's to Charity's
Garden, accompanied by a friend of Hughie's from the
mainland who was enjoying his first jaunt on the waters of
Newfoundland. The friend was Mr. Lewis Jones, and the
trip had been decided on between him and Inspector
Fitzgerald. It was quite natural, they had decided, for
Hughie Crocker to go to Charity's Garden to thank Mr.
Potter again for bringing the children home. Also he would
find the fishermen who had rescued them from the lonely
shore and offer them a suitable gift in the form of a large
basket of luscious imported fruit, a gift from the children's
grateful mother.

It had rained heavily in the late morning, but the skies
were clearing at noon. Tim had slept without even a dream
for nearly ten hours, and he had eaten a very big breakfast.

He felt fine. Last night he had been afraid that he and Meg and Mat would be shut out of everything further to do with Pirate's Cove, as they called it among themselves. The inspector wanted to keep them entirely out of it, but it was necessary for Mr. Lewis Jones to know the exact location of the cave. Inspector Fitzgerald couldn't have come on this trip; the inhabitants of Charity's Garden knew him and his official position. They would wonder and try to figure out why he had come.

Hughie handled the rented boat very well. Schoolteachers couldn't afford to own boats, he said, not when they owned cars. But he had spent a great many boyhood hours on boats. They made the trip to Charity's Garden in good time. It was interesting to see the place in daylight; only five tiny houses and a shop tucked into a wooded fold of the cliff, with gardens like handkerchiefs and the whole front of the settlement given over to what people here called "flakes." Flakes were platforms made of thin peeled poles, on which the cleaned and salted fish were laid to dry. The men brought the fish in and cut off their heads and cleaned them, and maybe they put them in the salt. They laid them out on the flakes. After that the wives and children turned the fish four or five times a day so that they wouldn't get sunburned. Everybody worked hard every minute when the cod were running. Mr. Potter had explained the process last night.

A low fog hung over the shore across the inlet, the shore where the cave was. That shore was veiled, hidden.

"Can we go back along there, Crocker?" Mr. Jones asked. "If the fog doesn't lift, we'll never be able to see a thing unless we're close in. Would that be a suspicious thing to do?"

101

"Oh, no. It would be the likely thing to do, showing strangers the island." Hughie slowed the boat, moved it in to the wharf of Charity's. He climbed out, tied it and reached back for the basket of fruit. Mr. Jones handed it to him carefully. He climbed out, and Tim followed.

Three women, seven children and three dogs came running down the wharf. One woman was carrying a small baby. Her face was dark with anxiety. The other women, too, looked fearful, unhappy. Behind them, coming from the store, Mr. Potter was hurrying down his steps to the wharf. They all waited, looking at the visitors without speaking. What were they waiting for?

Mr. Potter came all the way down the wharf. He said, "You've got news, then? There's been a report? Speak up, man, it's been a bad time. What's the news? Where are they, our boys? Come along, it's enough waitin' we've all had!"

"News?" Hughie repeated. He shook his head. "We've got no news, Mr. Potter. The boy came back to thank you for taking care of him and his brother and sister last night and to bring some fruit for the children."

"But the lads, man! That's what I'm talkin' about! Where are they? Surely there's been a report? Surely somebody picked them up, if they had an accident?" He waved his hand toward the women and children behind him. "It's their husbands and fathers. . . . We've been waitin' now all the long mornin'!"

Hughie gave Mr. Jones a quick glance. He said, "Your boys? Your men? Something has happened to them?"

"Well, to be sure, man! They went out last night to drop the nets, and they'd have been back before the dawnin'.

103

But they've not come back at all, not at all. I telyphoned to the radio station in St. John's, and to the newspaper, askin' for news. It's late, you know too well it is, and we've had not a word. Mary McGuire, she's lyin' up in her house sick near unto death, waitin' for her man to come home." His broad face was crumpling. "You must have word, man, you must have some word for us!"

Hughie said in a low voice, "This is bad. This is very bad."

"My son," Mr. Potter went on. "He's wan of thim. We've got only the four grown men except for me here in Charity's. They fish together. They'd just gone out last night when they spied the wee bonfire across on the shore, and they went across and got the childer. And then they went right out again, to lay the nets . . . and that's the last we know."

Mr. Jones said gently, "Where would they have been going to lay the nets?"

Mr. Potter looked at him as if he scarcely saw him. "Where they always go," he said. "Out along the shore a bit and then to the open water. Where they always go."

"And they should have been back early? Before dawn?"

Mr. Potter didn't answer. It was as if something terrible had finally come into his mind. He looked over the little huddle of women and children standing behind him, so quiet.

"It wasn't a stormy night," he said at last. "And they'd a good boat. A new boat, as I told the man from the *Telegram*. They'd just finished paintin' her. She was gay." His eyes went to Tim. "You remember, lad, a spankin' new boat, bright red, fit for anything. A good boat, and every wan o' them lived on the sea every day o' his life."

Mr. Jones said, "Was there a man here from the *Telegram?* You talked to him? When?"

"No, no," Mr. Potter said impatiently. "He telyphoned . . . away late it was, after I got back from takin' the childer to St. Joseph's. Not all the Outports has got telyphones, but we have. He said he'd heard about how the men from Charity's had rescued the mainland childer when they was lost, and he wanted the lads' names to put in the paper, and he wanted to talk to them on the phone to get a story. I give him the story. But they wasn't here, as any sane man ought to know. They was out layin' the nets."

"Did he ask about the boat?"

"He did that. I told him. A new boat, a bright red boat, and he could come and take a picture for the paper today, if he liked. The boys was proud of her." He looked at Mr. Jones. "It wasn't you that phoned? You're not the man from the *Telegram?*"

"No . . . I'm . . . just a visitor. Did you see the children's bonfire, Mr. Potter?"

"Not me. Not from here. The boys was almost over to the shore or they'd not have seen it themselves. An' that's another thing. It was my own boy, my Dan, who went ashore and tramped the fire out when they'd taken the childer inty the boat. He told me himself, and he always speaks the truth. So it wasn't that wee bonfire that spread and lay waste to that whole shore. If my Dan said he put the fire out, he did."

"Our bonfire?" Tim said. "Your Dan *did* put our fire out, Mr. Potter. I saw him. There wasn't a scrap of it left."

"There. I knew it. I was sure of it. So what did start the fire over there in the night? What did?"

105

Tim turned and looked across the inlet. The fog had lifted as they stood talking. On the far shore, there was nothing green left. All the trees were burned, black and fallen. There was nothing familiar about the headlands over which he and Meg and Mat had climbed and scrambled last night. There was only a stretch of burned-over shoreline. All the headlands looked alike now. And Meg's red wool markings? Their guided way back to the cave?

It was hard to get back into the boat and leave Charity's; it was terrible to leave people in such deep trouble and worry. Hughie turned the boat and hurried it over the water toward the other shore. Mr. Jones sat staring at that shore with a grim look on his face. Tim looked, too, looked and looked. Where had their bonfire been? Where was the cave? Which were the arms of land stretching out on either side of it and the fallen rock between them concealing the low archway? There were a dozen arms of land stretching out, and they all looked alike.

As they got near the shore, Hughie throttled down the boat. He said to Tim, "Well, boy?"

"All the trees are burned. Everything is changed. I . . . I can't see anything I remember. I can't."

Mr. Jones said to Hughie, "How do you get rid of four strong young men who can pinpoint a bonfire and give a location?"

Hughie looked at him for a long time. He took off his glasses. He said, "You put a few rifle bullets into the boat. Maybe into the men."

Tim looked up at Hughie. He couldn't believe what he was hearing. Mr. Jones didn't like what he had heard. His eyes were colder than ever. He said, "Explain."

"Well, it wouldn't have been hard, sir. If a man was so inclined. If a man knew that the four lads from Charity's who'd picked up the children had a new red boat, it wouldn't have been hard. He'd a boat himself, a small one — maybe he had a big motorboat too. There was still some low fog on the water. He'd set out, find the boat, get close enough to use the rifle — and then shoot. They'd have had to be a good long way from the shore, too far to swim. If he put holes in the boat, she'd sink, sir, and the men couldn't cling to her to save themselves. The water's desperate cold, here, the sea water. We've had icebergs right in St. John's, or as near the shore as they could come."

There was a long silence. The men looked at each other. There were things they didn't want to say. So, after a while, Tim said, "If that's what happened . . . then the man knew that we'd found the cave. Didn't he? Maybe he knew we marked the way back. So, if he set fire to the shore . . ." He stopped.

Mr. Jones said slowly, "I don't like this."

"Nor do I," said Hughie Crocker, shortly.

Tim said, "Maybe now we can't recognize the entrance to the cave from here. But surely if we started back from the road, up near the pond, we could find the back door to that tunnel. I'm sure we could."

Mr. Jones said evenly, "We'll find the sea entrance to the cave; we'll get boats searching along every foot of the shoreline. They'll find that long inlet and the open archway."

"If it's still open," Tim said anxiously. "He could have rolled more rocks down in front of it. He could have started a rock fall. Couldn't he? And the fire will have piled dead trees and brush over it. It might be very hard to find."

CHAPTER

11

THE THREE PATTERSON children were sitting on the stone wall at the corner of the entrance to the hotel parking area. They were trying to look absorbed in the view over the Narrows, in watching the wisps of mist swirl over the top of Signal Hall.

Meg said in a low voice, "Mom heard the broadcast about the missing fishermen. It scares her. She thinks it might have something to do with us — I can't see how. Surely they'll be all right? They were so nice. Danny Potter — he was the one who waded in to shore and carried me out to the boat. And Jake and Hal and the little one they called Sissle. They were so good to us, and then to have an accident — it doesn't seem a bit fair."

"I heard a part of a broadcast," Mat said. "They were saying that maybe the men saw the fire on shore and went

108

too far in to try to put it out, and a spark jumped to the boat. And maybe they're still somewhere along that shore, with their boat gone . . ."

"Hurt?" Meg said, her grey eyes big.

"Maybe hurt. I guess they'll send boats out to see if that's what happened."

Tim hadn't said anything about Hughie Crocker's mention of a rifle. He couldn't be right. Those four young men out on the dark water, laying their nets; pleased with themselves for having helped three lost kids, they'd been cheerful, healthy, happy men. They couldn't be dead.

If he mentioned that idea, Meg would cry. Mat, too, probably. And they weren't supposed to let on that they had anything much on their minds. They had to go around pretending to be dumb kids from the mainland, kids who had been lost and then found again, nothing else.

Mat said slowly, "That fire was queer. You can't get around it. Why did it have to happen just now? It started a few miles along the shore and raced along the edge of the cliffs, our cliffs. Just where we didn't need a fire. And it got started in the middle of the night. How? It wasn't started by lightning, there wasn't any lightning. They say it must have been a little picnic fire that somebody started yesterday and didn't really put out. It lingered on until it got into the trees on the edge of the cliffs." He looked at Tim straight, with his thoughtful eyes. "Do you believe that?"

There was a long silence. They were all turning things over in their minds, remembering, thinking. Wondering.

Meg said slowly, "If that man set the fire . . . if he did —" she stopped. "Did he see us tie the wool on bushes as we went away? Did he know we'd found the cave?"

109

Tim didn't answer. He didn't know the answer.

After a while Mat said slowly, "What I want to know is, who is that man? Where does he live, where does he keep his boat, where does he hide the treasure he takes out of the cave? He sure knows his way around. I bet he's some rich respectable businessman, right here in St. John's. He takes out a bunch of stuff once in a while, and he has some way to get it over to the mainland to sell it. He couldn't sell it here, he couldn't even let anybody here guess he had it. He has to be somebody respectable, maybe even important, so he can travel, not noticed. See what I mean?"

Meg shivered suddenly. "I don't like to think about him. He must be very smart, to figure things out so well. And if he set that fire, burning down trees, he's — he might be willing to do other things against the law. It's his treasure he cares about, only his treasure."

Tim had been going over the things that had happened inside the cave, trying to remember exactly what had happened. A small sharp picture came suddenly into his mind. "Meg — your red gloves! Didn't you lay them down on that old hearth when you were getting wood to start the fire? Didn't you leave them there?"

She stared at him, her big grey eyes wide and scared. She put her hand to her mouth. She went on staring at him.

Tim said steadily, "He goes into the cave in a boat at high tide, to get his load. We got out of there about six. He couldn't have taken a boat back in for about six hours again, on account of the tide. But suppose he went back at midnight for another load, and suppose his torch just happened to pick up those red gloves. . . ."

After a long time she said unevenly, "They wouldn't tell

110

him *when* we'd been there. I mean . . . the cave itself . . . he'd be furious enough about that, of course, but it's the treasure he must care about. As long as he didn't think we'd seen him there or knew about the treasure . . ." her voice died away.

"There was that fish I caught," Mat said darkly. "And my rod. And we'd got a fire ready to light, but we didn't light it. We didn't cook the fish. Wouldn't he say, why not? Wouldn't he wonder why we got scared off? Wouldn't he think we just might have seen him? Couldn't he tell if he looked at the treasure that we'd been into it?"

"He couldn't help knowing exactly who we were," Meg said. "It was on the radio, about our getting lost. And where we were lost. And where we are staying. He couldn't miss knowing exactly who we are."

"And," Mat said in a very soft voice, "if that's true . . . wouldn't he think we'd tell those four fishermen about the cave? Even if he couldn't tell whether we'd found the treasure, he'd be sure we'd have told the fishermen we'd found the cave. And if we had, they'd have been over there looking, the minute it was daylight. Anybody in Newfoundland would have gone there as fast as he could. A great big old pirate cave — of course the fishermen would have gone to investigate. So . . ." he stopped. He turned. His eyes met Tim's.

Tim took a long breath. "We're doing a lot of guessing. *I* think we better keep our mouths good and shut, especially around Mom. You know that? Good and shut."

As he spoke, his mother came from the hotel, with Peter and Patsy. The three children got up silently and went to meet her. She said, "Come along, you three. I want to go

111

see Hughie Crocker. There's something — I mean to say, I'm not sure we shouldn't cable to Labrador. Your father, he always knows what to do . . ." Her eyes went from one face to another. She wasn't missing anything. Not a thing.

Mr. and Mrs. Manren, smooth and elegant as ever, came out of the hotel on the way to their car. Mrs. Manren had her camera. Mr. Manren was carrying a sketching pad just like Meg's. They walked easily down the slope and paused. "Isn't it a heavenly day?" Mrs. Manren said brightly.

Mrs. Patterson looked at her. She said absently, "It's very pleasant."

"We're going to make a last visit to Portugal Cove. I want to get a few more pictures and Randle has to finish a sketch. We have to start home tomorrow, isn't that dreadful? It hasn't been half long enough. We haven't begun to see Newfoundland."

Mat said, "You see a lot of it driving across, don't you?"

"Yes, but the road is terribly bumpy and dusty most of the way, and when you have to try to find places to camp and worry about food, there isn't much time for enjoying the scenery. Anyway, there isn't much scenery in the middle of the island."

Mat said, "Places to camp? Aren't there motels?"

She laughed, her light tinkly laugh. "Oh, my, no, not enough," she said. "That's why we've got such a big station wagon. It's practically a trailer. It has beds to let down, one on each side, and a darling little set of kitchen things. You wouldn't think I was much of a cook, would you? The truth is, I'm not. But we can manage for two or three days."

The family stayed for supper at the Crockers, and Mollie Crocker cooked cod tongues for them and made a seal-flipper pie. The cod tongues were fresh, but the seal

112

flippers had been frozen in the winter when the seals were killed out on the ice. The food was interesting, and Meg asked all kinds of questions about it; but Tim for once didn't really care what he ate, and Mat was quiet, too. Mrs. Patterson had a private talk with her cousin Hugh. She still didn't know what to do, whether to cable their father to come to St. John's or let him finish his work without bothering him. It would only mean, she said, that if he came down now he'd just have to fly back in and stay longer later on. She tried hard not to let on that she was really frightened.

They got back to the hotel about eight o'clock. The television set in the lobby was turned to the news. The announcer was saying something about the four lost fishermen from Charity's. The Patterson children ran to the long sofa in front of the set and dropped down to hear what he was saying. The picture was of a stretch of lonely sea, and then a glimpse of Charity's Garden, set in its little fold of rock, and then of the opposite shore, with the ravages of the fire showing clearly. The announcer wasn't talking about the fire; the pictures were only background. He was saying that the men had been missing now for about twenty hours; their boat had headed out toward the open sea about eleven last night, but since then there had been no word of them at all. He ended, "It can only be presumed that they have met with a fatal accident."

Dick Ackley had been standing and listening. He sat down now beside Mat. He said, "A grim business. But that's Newfoundland. That really is Newfoundland."

"What do you think happened to them?" Tim asked. He glanced over Dick Ackley's face. It had a heavy look tonight; he was tired. Gloomy. Not natural.

"Well," he said, "a dozen things could have happened. If

113

there had been fog, they might have been run down by a big boat coming in, but there wasn't fog just then, nor any big boats coming in. It doesn't seem likely that they could have struck some sharp hidden reef; they were in waters they knew. They had a small engine. An engine can blow up. If they were a long way out and no boat to hang onto, they couldn't have made shore. Or — they might have made a fire for their mug-up, and the fire got away on them. That's a dangerous business, making a fire on board the boat. They get used to doing it, with a kind of stone hearth they make, but it's still dangerous."

"It was a new boat," Mat mentioned. "They were careful with it."

"Yes," Dick Ackley agreed. "So we hear. A new boat, painted red, and here are another four young men, reared up in Newfoundland, gone to a watery grave, who knows how? Maybe a small whale, strayed far inshore, rose up underneath the boat and sent it flying or broke it in two. Maybe anything. It's happened a thousand times." He turned and looked at the three of them. "They were the boys who rescued you from the shore?"

Nobody answered.

"Sorry," he said. "I'd rather forgotten that bit. Friends of yours. And you'd been on that shore that's burned now, hadn't you? Darn good thing you weren't there when the fire was raging. It looks as if it swept like lightning along that strip — there must have been a high wild wind. There usually is, up on the marshes. If it hadn't rained this morning, that fire might have spread inland, when it had burned its way along the shore past the marsh country."

Meg said, "What will happen to their families?"

115

"The fishermen's families? Over in Charity's Garden? Well, fortunately, since Newfoundland has joined with Canada, they won't starve. They'll get widows' pensions and the baby bonus and other government allowances. They'll get a living. Maybe even a better living than the men could have made fishing."

"They'd rather have the men," Meg said miserably. "They were nice men."

He looked at her oddly. "Probably you're right. Still, what's done is done. Isn't it?" He looked down at Mat. "How much longer are we to have the pleasure of your company here in St. John's?"

"Well, we don't exactly know," Mat said.

Tim said quickly, "We might go home any day now. Then Dad could come straight to Toronto and not come here at all."

"That would be disappointing for me. I'm looking forward to meeting him. I've explored a good deal of territory, but I've not spent much time in Labrador. Don't know much about the mineral possibilities. He does." He pulled out his battered package of cigarettes and lit one, as if he weren't exactly thinking about it. "Would you kids and your mother drive back to Port aux Basques? It's quite a trip."

"We haven't got our own car. That's a rented car Mom drives. We flew," Mat said.

"Oh, well, that's a good thing. It's heavy going in spots, especially when there is only one driver. Your mother isn't very big."

"But she's a good driver," Tim said.

"Yes, she's a very good driver. Careful. But she'd get

116

pretty tired doing that mileage to Port aux Basques. Five hundred and sixty-five miles, if my memory serves correctly."

"What happens to cars when they get to Port aux Basques?" Meg asked.

"They go by ferry over to Cape Breton. To the mainland. And then you'd still have about four days' driving before you'd reach Toronto, maybe five. A long trip. Flying is much easier."

What was he trying to say? Get out of here, get out fast? Tim looked at him incredulously. Dick Ackley? He thought back to the man in the cave, the man in the oilskins. He had been tall. Dick Ackley was tall. And he was smart.

Mat was thinking about Dick Ackley, too. He said, almost as if he weren't really thinking, "You said you got interested in the people of Newfoundland because you are a distant relative. Were you just making that up?"

Dick Ackley raised his eyebrows. "I said that, did I? Sounds boastful. I'll tell you — I'm not a Carew. I don't come down from the beautiful princess. I do come from somebody you may have heard of — Richard Hakluyt. Mean anything to you?"

Mat wrinkled his brows. "He wrote something about voyages."

"That's the man. The name was changed through the centuries from Hakluyt to Ackley. Hakluyt went to Oxford with Raleigh and Drake and Gilbert and the rest, but he wasn't a bold adventurer. He was a born reporter, see? What the other boys did fascinated him, but all he wanted to do was tell about it. That's me. Although — because practically all those people on the Welsh border had to be

117

related to some extent — I do have a bit of an interest, personal family interest, in that old pirate, Sir Henry Mainwaring. He brought his ship here a good deal. A smart old boy. Not really big, like Henry Morgan or Captain Kidd, but he did fairly well." He grinned. "Always thought I'd have liked to meet him, a swashbuckling type if ever there was one. Came from Cheshire, within a few miles of the Hakluyts."

"Sir Henry *who?*" Mat repeated. His eyes were startled.

"Mainwaring. I'm saying it properly, the way it's said in England, Mannering. It's spelled Main-waring. You'll see it in the books, if you look for it."

Tim asked quickly, "Was he the last pirate who ever came to Newfoundland?"

Dick Ackley gave him a quick glance. "You especially interested in pirates, Tim?"

"Why not? Isn't everybody?" Tim got up. "We'd better go to bed," he said. "Mat, come on."

Dick Ackley said heartily, "That's for me, too. I wrote all night, last night. Got an inspiration and settled right into it." He put a hand on Tim's shoulder. "Well, however you go home, you three, I wish you a safe journey."

Mat said easily, "How are you going home, when you go? Did you fly over?"

"Yes, but I don't care too much for flying. Too quick. I'm going back by boat."

"Then you'll have to drive to Port aux Basques."

"I would if I weren't lucky. I have a friend with a small yacht. He's going to put in here one day soon and I'll go back with him."

CHAPTER
12

TIM AND MAT talked for a long time that night after their light was out. They kept their voices low, so that nobody would know they were talking.

They got up early, before their mother and Meg and the twins were up. They went down and had breakfast as soon as the dining room opened. The Manrens had breakfast, too. And afterwards, when the boys went out to the lobby, they saw that all the Manren baggage was stacked there, and two bellboys were waiting to take it down to the car.

The Manrens came from the dining room. Mr. Manren was smiling. He wasn't much of a smiler. He was trying to be nice while he said good-bye to people. The hotel manager himself came out to talk to him and shake hands. He said, "I'm sorry you aren't staying, Mr. Manren. We'd expected you to be here all summer. It's too bad you have to go."

"Well, you know how these things are," Mr. Manren said pleasantly. "Things happen. Something came up that I have to attend to in my business. We're sorry too."

"But we've had a lovely time," Mrs. Manren said quickly. "You've been awfully good to us. We'll never forget. We'll come back as soon as we can. We might even be able to come back again this summer, mightn't we, Randle?"

"Oh, I doubt that," he said. "But next summer, for sure." He turned to Tim and Mat. He put out his hand. "Have to say good-bye to you boys, too," he said. "I'd like to have met your father. Too bad he had to be in Labrador. I imagine he'll be along soon, too, and I'll miss him."

"He might," Tim said.

"He's got a fine reputation," Mr. Manren said. "Well, good-bye, both of you." He reached into his pocket and brought out a crisp new ten-dollar bill. "I wish you'd buy some flowers for your mother with this," he said. "We didn't get to see much of her. Give her our best wishes and say good-bye for us, won't you?"

"Oh, yes, do," Mrs. Manren said in her gushing way.

Tim held the money by the corner. People didn't give him money. Still, flowers for his mother. . . . He folded it slowly and put it into his pocket.

The bellboys took the luggage down and packed it into the car. A waiter came hurrying from the dining room with a big picnic basket. It looked heavy. He took it down to the car. The Manrens got in and the car drove away. Old Pete, the head bellboy, came up the stairs, puffing a little. He said, "She talked about cookin', gettin' over to Port aux Basques. Cookin'! They about bought out the delicatessen store yestiddy, and they got enough stuff packed in ice in that basket to get 'em clear to Halifax even if they never hit an eatin' place."

The lobby was empty. Tim looked at Mat. Mat looked back at him. "Well?" Tim said.

"Well, what have we got to lose?"

They went into the elevator and up to the second floor. They walked along to Room 206. They knocked. Mr. Jones opened the door. He looked surprised to see them. He was having breakfast in his room, and Inspector Fitzgerald was with him. There was a big stack of papers on the desk, as if they had already been working on something, whatever people in police jobs had to work at. Files, reports, pictures.

"Good morning," Mr. Jones said. "Can I do something for you?"

Mat said in a low voice, "We thought of a few things we ought to tell you about."

He opened the door wide. "Come in." He looked at them anxiously. "Nothing has happened to worry you? You haven't been talking to anyone, I'm sure. You've got something on your minds?"

They went in and sat down side by side on the couch under the window. Inspector Fitzgerald finished his coffee. Mr. Jones lifted his cup, took a last sip and then pushed the table toward the door. He sat down and waited.

It was Mat who said, "We haven't told anybody anything. But we think somebody was trying to get us to talk about things. Last night."

"Who, Mat?"

"Mr. Dick Ackley. He was anxious to know when we were

121

going home, and how, and about our father and things like that. He said a lot of things that made us think." Mat got a little pink. "We talked about it after we went to bed."

Mr. Jones glanced at Inspector Fitzgerald. It was only the flick of an eye. "Mr. Dick Ackley," he repeated politely.

"Well," Mat insisted, "you see, if that cave was really Sir Henry Mainwaring's big cave . . . well, Mr. Ackley is a kind of a relative of Sir Henry Mainwaring. He says so himself."

Mr. Jones looked up at him. "And it was Sir Henry Mainwaring who left the treasure in his old cave?" His voice was odd.

Tim spoke up. "When you were looking at one of the coins we brought back, you said 1753. So we know the treasure couldn't have been Sir Henry Mainwaring's. But the cave might have been."

"I see."

"Somebody could have known about the cave, somebody in the family. And then — well, somebody along the line got his hands on another treasure and hid it in the cave." He took a deep breath. "The Cocos Island treasure, sir. The date would be all right for that. We looked it up. The — well, the Loot of Lima."

Mr. Jones sat absolutely still. His face did not change. After a while he said, softly, "I don't think I would explore that idea too far, Tim, even in your own mind. I hope you understand me."

Tim's heart jumped. So, had he been right? The Cocos Island treasure? The Loot of Lima? That's really what they might have found?

He said, "We can hold our tongues. But what we wanted to say — you want to get to that cave fast. I know. You don't want anybody to know you're looking for it. So there's only the back door."

Neither man spoke.

"We want that cave found, too," Tim went on. "Our mother is getting very worried. She is mentioning taking us home. She is thinking about cabling for our father. But we figure — well, taking us home isn't going to do any good if that man knows who we are and if he knows that we know anything. If he saw us tie that red wool to mark a path, he knows we know something. The fishermen would be able to say just where our bonfire was, but the fishermen are gone. There's only us to help. And we think the only way we can help is to find that back door again."

Mr. Jones said nothing.

After a long minute Inspector Fitzgerald said, "The lad's right, sir. He's got it all in a nutshell."

Mr. Jones lifted his head. "This needs careful consideration," he said. "It needs the greatest consideration." He looked at Mat and then at Tim. "Thank you," he said. "When we can make a few decisions we shall get in touch with you."

❖   ❖   ❖

An hour later, they were all getting ready for church. Mat, putting on his white shirt and tie, said, "You don't really think we're in danger, do you, Tim?"

"The sooner we find that back door, the better I'll feel," Tim said. "You read about bank robbers shooting people for a few thousand dollars . . . if we're the only people who know about the cave . . . we might have told those fishermen, but they're probably dead. Maybe the man already knows we didn't tell Mr. Potter. Mr. Potter's a great talker.

He'd have let on some way if he knew. Dick Ackley's found out we're kind of close-mouthed about some things, the way Dad has taught us to be. Maybe he thinks we won't tell anybody but Dad about the cave. He could figure it that way. Mr. Ackley was pretty anxious to find out when Dad was coming, wasn't he?"

"Well, he kind of wiggled around the question," Mat agreed.

"I bet that's the score. He doesn't know we know about the treasure, only the cave. He thinks we won't tell anybody but Dad about the cave and the minute Dad comes, he'll take charge and the whole thing will come out in the open, but with lots of police taking care of things. He knows that Dad would have things done right. He knows if Dad comes, he'll lose all the rest of the treasure. He might not get caught himself. But then again, he must have the gold he's already taken hidden away somewhere, and if the police get into the story, he'd know they'd find it. So if it's Dad he's worrying about . . ." Tim shook his head. He tied the lace on his shoe. Leather shoes felt awful after wearing rubber-soled shoes all summer. "Whatever you do, don't tell Mom. She can't do anything."

"What do you take me for?" Mat said indignantly, and put on his blue coat. He looked scrubbed and polished, the way their mother always wanted them to look when they went to church.

The twins were ready, Peter in a blue linen suit and Patsy in a pink linen dress with a little round white hat. They were very nice twins, even if a person couldn't help wishing they'd hurry up and get some sense. They got into everything, faster than the speed of lightning, and it took about four people to keep them from killing themselves at least once a day. They ran out in front of cars, they walked up to strange animals, they ran down steep hills as fast as they could go, they fell into any stretch of water they could find, they leaned out of high windows and they talked to strangers when nobody was holding them by the hand or the shirttail.

Mrs. Patterson was ready, too, in the pale yellow dress that matched her hair, with a pale yellow hat and white gloves. Meg looked unfamiliar in a new blue dress with a white collar and a round white hat quite a bit like Patsy's, and she was wearing gloves, too, and carrying a purse.

Mrs. Patterson's eyes went over the two boys. She smiled. "You look perfect," she said. She glanced at the clock. "We'll have to hurry a little, we haven't much time."

They went downstairs, and at the hotel door Meg and Mat each took a twin firmly by the hand, to stand and wait for the car. Tim went around to the parking area with his mother. He wished that he could drive, but officially it would be almost three years before he could get a permit. He *could* drive, as far as that went; his father had taught him long ago, and inside the fences at Echo Valley he drove all the time. But he could never go an inch out on the public road, even over to Gorrie's Corner to get the mail. He was as tall as his mother, now, even a little taller; he was stronger, too. It wouldn't have tired him to drive, as it did her. But still, they wouldn't let him.

He got into the front seat beside her. She turned the car, and they went along the level alley leading out to the street. The others were waiting right at the corner, and Mat opened the door of the back seat while Meg and the twins

125

got in. They had to go down the steep hill to Water Street and then out along Water Street for a good many blocks to get to their church.

Mrs. Patterson turned the car down the hill. Tim knew that she didn't like that hill. It was only a short hill, but it really was very steep, and if the car got away on you, you would dash straight down and probably crash through the houses beside the wharf and plunge right into the deep water.

The car moved forward. Something was wrong. Tim saw his mother's lips tighten. She put her foot down on the brake pedal, and Tim saw that the pedal was loose and slack. The car began to move; it wasn't a big heavy car, but it was heavy enough so that once it got underway . . .

Mrs. Patterson said in an agonized voice, "Tim . . . the children . . . the brakes . . ."

He knew what to do. He reached over, took the wheel from her and swung the car away around to the left. It dived up onto the curb. It rushed straight into the wide glass window of the small real estate building there on the side hill. It broke the window, but it stopped. The windshield wasn't broken, nothing was broken except that glass window.

Mrs. Patterson put her face down into her hands. She said in a wretched voice, "The brakes wouldn't work at all. They wouldn't work at all."

In the back seat, Meg had climbed out and was taking the twins, absolutely silent, out of the car. Mat said, "Jeepers, that was close," in a small voice.

People came running. There hadn't been anybody you could see on the streets, but suddenly there were a dozen

people all around them; the bellboys from the hotel, three or four men who had been down on the wharf, two very stout old women all dressed up on their way to the cathedral. And, almost first of them all, a policeman.

Tim said, "The brakes wouldn't work. My mother couldn't get them to work. I twisted the wheel. I'm sorry about the window."

The policeman looked at the car. It was new, shiny. He said, "That's a rented car, to be sure. Good people. They keep their cars in order, we don't have a bit of trouble with them. What's your name, Ma'am?"

Mrs. Patterson lifted her head. "I'm Mrs. Ben Patterson. These are my children. We're living in the hotel. What my boy says is true. The brakes wouldn't take hold at all. If he hadn't twisted the wheel, we'd have gone straight down the hill and crashed through those little buildings into the water, Officer. This is true."

He wrote in his notebook. He said "It's not a nice thought, Ma'am. You go along back to the hotel. This'll be looked into immedjit. I can promise you that. Brakes has to work. There's somebody in for a good wiggin', I can promise you that."

They went back to the hotel. They went upstairs in the elevator, nobody saying anything, not even the twins. Inside their own sitting room, Mrs. Patterson stood and looked at the three older children, at Meg and Tim and Mat.

She said, "Do you think that was accidental? Do you?"

CHAPTER

13

THEY WERE ALL BACK on the edge of the marshes again; Tim
and Mat and Meg and Pat Kennedy and Hughie Crocker
and Tom Merrick, and with them were Mr. Lewis Jones
and Inspector Fitzgerald. They had driven out in three cars;
and the cars sat now on the road, with two steady-eyed
young policemen standing beside them, watching everywhere. Back in St. John's, Dick Ackley might or might not
know it, but there were probably half a dozen men keeping
an eye on him or asking questions about him of everyone
who knew him. They hadn't seen him this morning; he
hadn't come down to breakfast. He hadn't come down to go
to church. He was in his room, all right, because the maid
had used her passkey and walked in, as if she thought he
had gone out. He was in bed.

Well, he had said he was tired. He had been writing all
night, he said, on Friday night. Had he?

And what about Saturday night?

The brakes of the Patterson car had been tampered with. The brake fluid was all drained out. They'd held only for that instant when Mrs. Patterson had stopped the car at the corner of the alley to let the children climb in. If the car had once gathered any speed at all, if Tim hadn't twisted the wheel almost before he thought of doing it, they might all have been at the bottom of the sea; and who would then have known, for a long time, anyway, that the brakes had been deliberately damaged. Who would have thought to look for such a thing — or so the man who had damaged them would think. If the children hadn't talked, and he didn't know they had, nobody would suspect such a terrible thing. Nobody would ever guess that the accident was anything but what might happen to a woman driving with a carload of children to distract her attention and make her do the wrong thing.

The wind was strong again, up here at the top of the slope. It tore at them just as it had torn at them on Friday, when they had started over the path to the pond.

"Well, Tim?" said the inspector. "Meg? Mat?"

Meg said, "Pat Kennedy was the last on the path. He knows right where he and Mat were."

Pat Kennedy's face was drawn, unhappy. He said, "Yes, I know. And why wasn't I usin' my noggin on Friday night? This is all my fault."

"The fog was terrible," Meg said simply. "Mat fell forward and his face was squashed into the marsh. He couldn't say a word. He couldn't get up. And you couldn't have seen him, Pat."

"Where did this happen exactly?" Inspector Fitzgerald asked.

Pat walked to a spot just beyond the beginning of the rocky slope that went down to the road. He stepped into the marsh; he stood on the narrow wet path with the beautiful little marsh plants growing like a deep thick spongy rug all around his feet. Bake-apple, and partridge berry, and the pitcher plant waiting with its hungry mouth for insects to fly in and be gobbled up. "Just here," he said. "I don't know where the lad fell, sir. But not far back. I'd been talkin' to him all the way. He's a bright talker. He makes fun. Not more than a foot or two back."

"Mat?"

Mat went to Pat. He looked down at the path. There was a big tussock right in the middle of it. Mat said, "I think that's what I fell over. You see how the path goes around it? I didn't go around it. I fell flat."

Meg and Tim went to him. This was right. They weren't more than three steps off the rock. Tim went to the spot where Mat thought he had fallen and then stepped backward, as he had on Friday night, to the rock. "We started from here," he said. "I think we went down the slope a little way. A few feet. And then we joined hands, and we edged to the left."

"Not to the left," Hughie Crocker said. "If you'd gone to the left, Tim, you'd never have crossed the road. It takes a deep bend just there at the beginning of the rise. You *had* to cross the road. The sea isn't on this side, it's over there, to the south."

"But we were facing the road," Tim said. "We could hear the cars when they drove off. We were facing the road, and then we edged along the rock to the left, all together."

Tom Merrick said in his gentle way, "You got turned around, lad. It's a thing can happen to anyone in the fog.

You must have gone to the right. See, the top of the rise is there to the right. You edged along this rim of rock, and you got to the road; and it's rough there, with stones on it, to be sure. You had to go that way. You'd never have got down to the sea going to the left."

Tim felt stubborn, but he had to be wrong. The sea *was* on the south side of the road, and a good long way, too. That underground passage they had followed — how long had it been? Not all that long. Not a mile, not even half a mile.

"Well," he said. "Come on, you two." He led the way, walking slowly and carefully to the right, along the rim of rock. Rock was rock. It wasn't slippery and dangerous, now in the bright afternoon sun. It seemed a lot shorter; they could move faster.

The edge of the rock took them to the road, rising steeply here. It was rough. It did have stones on it. But he couldn't remember the feel of it under his feet. Every step of that walk on Friday night was in his mind, every step. There had not been even fifteen feet of this kind of smooth going.

He stopped. He looked at Meg and Mat. They both shook their heads. "This isn't the way we came, sir," Tim said flatly. "It isn't."

The whole group stood silent, gazing out over the marshes. Off on the horizon, the ocean was in sight. The water glittered in the sun. It was south; that was true. But they hadn't gone south to get to it.

"There isn't any big heap of stones over there," Tim said. "You can see a long way. And doesn't the marsh begin right here on the edge of the road? We didn't step back into the marsh. We knew better. We stayed on rock all the way."

It was Mat who said in a small voice, "That cave was big. It was very big. And it's at the end of a very long inlet. We might be standing right on top of the cave, at the end of a very long inlet. The inlet might come in under the road."

"Sure, the boy makes sense," Pat said. He turned and looked the other way, to the left. There was no heap of stones in sight there, either. He looked at Inspector Fitzgerald. "Let the boy try it his way, sir. There's instinct, you know that. The fishermen have to use it when they go out in the fog and there's not a thing to steer by."

Mr. Jones said, "Tim, do it your own way. We'll follow."

The three children went back to the starting point. This time they turned left, edging along the rock. They moved on and on . . . and on.

There were plenty of piles of stones here, when you got quite a way from the road. Lots of them, big stones, sticking up into the air. How could anybody know which one they had come to? They all looked alike. Just big stones, piled helter-skelter. Boulders, poking up out of the solid rock.

Tim stopped helplessly. "It's different, in daylight, and no fog. We seemed to go on for so long. We were scared, and it was cold. It was very cold. That's why we looked for some big rocks, for a shelter." He stared at a big boulder not far ahead. "What's on the other side of that one?" He went to see. Everyone went with him.

It wasn't right. The other side of the boulder had a sort of cleft in it, all right, but there was a tree growing in the cleft. They couldn't have made their way past it. It was quite a big tree, and it filled the cleft completely. They all looked at it, and then went on to the next heap of boulders.

Nothing was right. There just wasn't any pile of rocks

133

here with a crevice in the far side, a crevice opening to a path leading down. There just wasn't.

After a long time, when every pile of rocks within half a mile had been gone over, it looked hopeless.

"It's a good thing we took back those samples," Mat said. "They wouldn't believe us at all if we hadn't."

"But we *didn't* make up a story," Tim said. He began to think. He began to go over every single thing he could remember. He turned his mind back to Friday night, to the number of steps they had taken, to the time it had taken to get so cold, to everything. He turned and looked again at the piles of rock. His eyes went over Mr. Lewis Jones' thoughtful face, with a look of trouble on it; Inspector Fitzgerald's eyes didn't say anything; but Pat Kennedy and Hughie Crocker and Tom Merrick wouldn't really look at him. So people thought they were lying, he and Meg and Mat. Lying. They thought that if there was a cave — if that wasn't a big lie too — then the three had likely found it by way of the shore. The stairway and the underground passage were just like something out of *Alice in Wonderland*.

While he was thinking, angry, a picture began to form in his mind. He had seen something today that wasn't right. It was something to do with his Scout woodcraft. He turned it over and over in his mind, standing there on the rock, staring out toward the far distant gleam of the sea.

"Well," Mr. Jones said slowly, "I suppose we had better go back to town."

Tim heard him, but he didn't pay any attention. Instead he turned and ran toward one heap of boulders. Not the first heap, not the one right on the edge of the rock slope. They had slipped and slithered down a good many steps

135

from that rim, making sure they wouldn't step into the marsh at the top. The other heap, down below the edge. He put his hands against the big flat boulder facing him and then edged on around it. And this was the rock with the cleft in it, and the tree growing in the cleft, a biggish tree, green and healthy, crowded into the cleft. He stood looking at it. He took a long breath. He said, "Inspector Fitzgerald —"

They were all beside him in half a second. He pointed. "Look!" he said. "That tree is supposed to be growing inside that cleft. If it grew there, it's been there a long time. Then why are some of the branches too long? The rock would have stopped them. They're too long, and they're bent back. I don't think that tree is really growing in that rock. I don't."

It was Pat Kennedy who stepped forward and Tom Merrick, tall and strong, behind him. They put their hands together on the trunk of the tree. None of the trees in Newfoundland was very big. The trunk of this one wasn't more than eight inches thick. The two men pulled at it strongly, and it moved. Inspector Fitzgerald and Hughie Crocker and Lewis Jones were all beside them in no time, trying to find places for their hands.

It didn't take long.

The tree lay beside the boulders. It hadn't been growing in the cleft. It had been cut close to the roots and then jammed into the cleft. There was a lot of brush jammed into the cleft, too, put there before the tree had been put there. The men pulled the brush away.

"Well," Mat said comfortably, "there's the back door. There it is."

CHAPTER

14

IT WAS ALMOST DARK when they returned to the hotel that Sunday night. But Mrs. Patterson knew that everything was all right. She had been officially notified.

The trip down to the cave had been very exciting, but a lot farther than the children had remembered. All the men were silent, following along, each one full of his own thoughts. They found the end of the passageway and moved out into the vast empty cavern. Meg's gloves were no longer on the fireplace ledge.

The tide was just beginning to come in. The sand in the bottom of the cave was still dry, and Tim was able to show the men where to go to get to the ledge leading up to the treasure room. He and Meg and Mat went up there again, to see it for the last time.

Mr. Lewis Jones was the one who began checking it all

over. Inspector Fitzgerald had other things to think about. He set Hugh Crocker and Pat Kennedy and Tom Merrick, along with himself, to clearing away the burned brush and debris from in front of the archway of the cave. They had to hurry, to do it before the tide really came in. Once outside, Inspector Fitzgerald used a whistle, and almost like magic a police boat was racing in to shore. The boat carried a police radio. It sent a message to Mrs. Patterson and more messages to the men who were watching Mr. Dick Ackley. Tim heard the inspector's orders.

The tide was coming into the cave, and the men had to work in water. The police boat could not get under the archway. But before the tide had come in too far, Pat and Tom and Hughie and the inspector and Mr. Jones had carried the heavy boxes out to the sand beyond the archway, and they were loaded into the boat. There were seventeen boxes. Most of the boxes were alike, of heavy brass-bound leather. They would be the ones holding the gold bars. There were three or four different boxes, one like a small humpbacked trunk. Inside it now was the leather box from which the children had taken the coins and the jewelled statuette.

Mr. Jones wouldn't leave the treasure for a single moment. When it was being loaded into the boat, he stood beside it. He got into the boat with it. Those boxes held the lives of a great many people; men who had been killed for what was in them, pirates and good people alike. Who knew what the treasure in those old boxes really meant? Who could ever know?

The children were taken back to St. Joseph's on the police boat too. Inspector Fitzgerald looked grim; he wasn't going to let them out of his sight for an instant. Anyone who knew about this awful treasure had to be watched. Gold could turn any man into a kind of animal, couldn't it?

Mr. Jones and the inspector went with the police truck that unloaded the boat. It was Sunday evening, there weren't any people down on the wharf, or if there had been, they had been cleared away, and a ring of policemen had moved in. The truck came quietly, took the boxes, and went away quietly, to some place known only to Mr. Jones and the inspector. The treasure would be well guarded. Tim had a feeling that these men wanted nothing so much in the world as to have that treacherous stuff given back safely to whoever owned it, if anyone did.

Mr. Dick Ackley was in the hotel lobby. His eyes were stormy, his hair was wild, as if he had run his hands through it a hundred times. There were three policemen with him. There was nobody else in the lobby; if there were any tourists staying in the hotel they were still out seeing the country. If there were any local people or hotel staff, it looked as if the policemen had shut them away behind doors.

Dick Ackley faced the inspector. He said angrily, "I want to know the meaning of this, Fitzgerald. For the last five hours I've been some kind of prisoner. These men don't arrest me, for whatever trumped-up charge you've got in mind, they just say I have to wait until you come. What in the name of the devil have I done? What's going on here? I don't get it. Why am I being fenced in as if I were a mad bull? I want to know. I want to know this instant."

"Yes, of course," the inspector said slowly. "I've got to ask you some questions, Mr. Ackley. You've been coming to

Newfoundland for a few summers — four or five, anyway. Why?"

"Why? Coming to Newfoundland? I happen to like the country. I'm writing a book about it, maybe half a dozen books. There are more than half a dozen books waiting to be written. Is this a crime? What am I supposed to be doing that's wrong?"

The inspector said solidly, "Where were you on Friday night?"

"Friday night? Friday? The night the kids were lost . . . and Potter brought them home? I was here. I was in the lobby when Mrs. Patterson received the phone call from them." He stopped. He stared at the inspector.

"And then?"

"I went to my room and wrote all night. I got a new idea, from the kids being lost. Something clicked. I got two chapters done. I wrote until daylight."

"You can't prove that, can you?"

Dick Ackley looked at him grimly. "No, I can't prove it. I wanted coffee, a couple of times, but there's no room service in this place at night. I can't prove it. Where was I supposed to be? Did anybody say they saw me somewhere else?"

"Mr. Ackley, have you a rifle?"

"Have I a *what*? Of course I've got a rifle. I go hunting. I've got a rifle, and I've got a permit for it. Like a thousand other people who come here hunting. What's that got to do with anything?"

The inspector looked tired. He said carefully, "And where were you *last* night, sir?"

Dick Ackley stared at him. He said, "I was in bed." He

141

looked at Tim and Meg and Mat. He said, "You kids are mixed up in whatever this is, up to your necks. I thought you were my pals. Did you get some crazy ideas in your head about me? Did you get some addlepated notions, who could even guess what, out of the history I was giving you? I don't get it. Where was I supposed to be last night?"

The inspector said gently, "Someone went into the hotel parking place last night and drained the brake fluid out of Mrs. Patterson's car. It was quite out of control, this morning. When she turned down the hill, the brakes wouldn't work. It was only because the lad here twisted the wheel very fast that they were saved from rushing down the hill, maybe from plunging into the sea."

Dick Ackley was as white as a ghost. He sat down in a red leather chair. He said, "You think I could have done that? You think . . . look, I'm Dick Ackley. I'm a writer I'm not a storybook villain. Why would I want to do a fearful thing like that? You're talking about murder, man! You're accusing me of murder."

"No, not yet. I'm trying to get to the bottom of a few very confused matters." He stopped. He said, "Mr. Ackley, did you ever, in your travelling about Newfoundland, asking questions, did you ever come upon the old legend of Sir Henry Mainwaring's cave?"

Dick Ackley didn't answer. He just sat.

"The boys here say that you told them you were a relative of Sir Henry Mainwaring. The old pirate. You know all about him. Is this true?"

After a long time Dick Ackley said, "So that's it. Sir Henry Mainwaring's cave. It's been found, then? It really existed? It's been found, and there was something important in it?"

"It's been found. There was something important in it. There was probably originally a great deal more, but it looks as if the horde had been systematically pilfered for a good many years. There is nothing in the cave now. It's as empty as a broken eggshell. We've taken what was there and put it in a very safe place. There'll be no more pilfering."

Dick Ackley looked at Meg and Mat and Tim. He said slowly, "So, you found it. Yes, it would happen that way. Hundreds of people have spent years looking for that old lost cave. They've stopped believing it ever existed. But you found it." He stopped. He said, "Yes, old Sir Henry was an ancestor of mine — a great-great-uncle about twenty times removed. Not what you call a direct line. I'm a lot closer to Richard Hakluyt, who wrote a lot of exciting stuff about early Newfoundland. That's what runs in my blood, writing about strange new places." He paced up and down the floor. "Sir Henry Mainwaring. Suppose when he went back to England he had among his gear a map showing that cave? Suppose he had. Suppose three or four generations later, when old Sir Henry's pirate gold was all spent, a grandson or a great-grandson found the map and came and settled in Newfoundland — maybe not meaning to settle, only intending to find the cave and see whether anything had been left in it? He didn't have any money. He could have had a hard time here, early days. Suppose he found the cave — empty, bare. Not a bit of red gold anywhere in it. Or, suppose there was a little horde — no, that won't do. He'd have spent it."

"And what might you be gettin' at, sir?" The inspector asked carefully.

"Well, I guess I'm writing a blood-and-thunder adventure story," Dick Ackley said. "But it could have happened just that way. The English boy, penniless, gets out there — no gold. He has to take what comes, bitter bread. Suppose he marries a Newfoundland girl and has sons. He'd show them the cave, wouldn't he? And they would show *their* sons, always keeping very, very quiet because there might just be a very secret little room that no one had yet discovered. And then . . ."

"And then?"

"Well, at some point . . ." he said slowly, "at some point a watchful young Mainwaring sees a chance to replenish the loot. I've — I've been interested in that mysterious cabin boy who was mixed up with the Loot of Lima. The boys know what I mean, I told them about that loot. Suppose he was a Mainwaring? Reared up in Newfoundland, Inspector? Suppose he managed to get his hands on that Loot of Lima. *Somebody* got it. Suppose he brought it back here by devious means and hid it. And then he took a big load of it away somewhere, likely to New England. He settled there, a rich man. But the secret again was kept in the family so that when funds got low, one by one the generations could come back here and get more." He said very slowly, "And they are careful men, but after a while . . . well, what? What happened?" He stopped and looked straight into Tim's eyes. "After a while, one of these cautious secretive careful men might marry himself a greedy young wife." He laughed. "You know, when you read the name, it's *Main waring*. But it isn't spoken that way, not in England. It's Mannering. Mannering."

There was a silence. Then Mat said, "And they don't

144

pronounce the *g* on the end of a word in Newfoundland, do they? So it wouldn't even be Mannering. It would be Mannerin. Or . . ." He stopped too. He and Dick Ackley, the two with imaginations, stood looking at each other for a long time. Then Mat said, "Maybe we know where the gold is."

Dick Ackley said soberly, "Thinking everything over, I guess we do. I'm a fool. You know what the basic Mainwaring Christian name was? For generations. Randal. She called him Randle, I heard her. With my own two little ears. I saw it in the hotel cards. Randle Manren. Randal Mainwaring, Inspector. The man with the expensive wife and the rich clothes and the king-sized station wagon — now on his way to Port aux Basques, to the mainland, by way of the Cape Breton ferry. And once on the mainland — where? Another car, quick. A fine secret hideaway. No?"

"Not yet," the inspector said flatly. "We've a good bit of checking to do first. A good bit. You'll kindly answer me all my questions, Mr. Ackley, before we start off on another trail. I never was one to like red herrings."

He didn't start asking questions right away. He sent two of the younger policemen away to check on the Manrens. They were to find out all kinds of things; if Mr. Manren had ever been in Newfoundland before; if he showed any special knowledge of the island; how long he had been married; where he came from; all about his business back in New York. A lot of those questions would have to be asked of the New York police. It might take a long time. Tim found himself getting very troubled. When was that station wagon supposed to catch the ferry? How soon?

But some of the answers that lay right here in Newfoundland seemed to fill in a lot of gaps for the inspector. Yes, Mr. Manren had been in Newfoundland before. He came about once every five years. This was the first time he had brought a wife along. He seemed to know the island; never asked any questions, anyway. The inspector listened; he kept a lot of the answers to himself. He went away and talked on the telephone five or six times.

He wasn't only checking on Mr. and Mrs. Manren. He was checking on Dick Ackley.

Finally he came back. He said slowly, "Mind, there's not a thing settled yet. You've a great gift of gab, Mr. Ackley, and I've no doubt you've been thinkin' about this story for a good while. I've no doubt at all. But it doesn't look as if you are the guilty man. There's folk that know where you were, bits and pieces of time, last night and the night before. There's a lot of other folk that speak well of you. You can't fool a real down-to-earth Newfoundlander, not about a man's character, and nobody thinks you're anything but what you say you are. Still and all, you're not to leave the hotel. Stay put, sir, and we'll go along with the checking. It's a bad thing to accuse anyone of what we think our man is guilty of. It's not just the gold — that's dishonest enough, likely, although there's barely a mother's son of a Newfoundlander who wouldn't be tryin' to get his hands on a bit of it, now. No, it's not just the gold. It's murder. It's attempted murder, anyway, and it looks as if those four lads from Charity . . ." he stopped. "Well, that's it," he said. "Just don't be leavin' the hotel."

"Wouldn't think of it for a minute," Dick Ackley answered. "This is the middle of the web, right now, isn't it? I'll be right here, Inspector Fitzgerald. You couldn't shake me off if you tried."

146

The telephone rang again, for the inspector. He was gone a long time; maybe he wasn't coming back. He had plenty of other business to attend to in St. John's.

Mat whispered to Tim, "I'm nervous."

"The Manrens?"

"If they're really driving that long slow road to Port aux Basques, they must be awfully sure of themselves, Tim. Mustn't they?"

"Well," Tim said slowly, "who is there for them to be afraid of? If our car had crashed . . ." he stopped. It was a queer thing, to try to think that their car might really have crashed.

"And the fishermen?" Mat muttered. "What happened to them? They would know exactly where our bonfire was. If we'd told them about the cave and how far we had walked before we lit the signal fire — Tim, what about the fishermen?"

Tim still couldn't mention what Hughie Crocker had said. If there had been rifle bullets cutting into that little brave red boat in the night, it was their fault, wasn't it? If the fishermen were dead, those four kind young men, it would always be something dreadful to remember. The Pattersons would be responsible for those four deaths. It was too big a load to want to look at. He sat filled with dumb misery, knowing that he could never, never talk about this to anyone.

The inspector came back. His broad kindly face was glowing. He sat down in a chair facing the boys. He said, "It's good news I've got for you. They'll soon have it on the picture. It's good news for us, too, in the police, because now we've got witnesses. Believe it or not, lads, we've got living witnesses."

147

Dick Ackley said quickly, "The fishermen . . . they're safe?"

"They are indeed."

Tim felt a huge lump coming up in his throat. He wouldn't cry for anything, never. But he couldn't have said a word. Nobody noticed; they were all staring at Inspector Fitzgerald.

"The crazy man went after them in his boat," the inspector said. "It's a boat they all know. It belongs to Harry Dell of St. Joseph's, a big, very speedy motor launch. He rents it, summers. He knows very well whom he rented it to this summer — the man we're after, Manren. The boys recognized the boat, and that would have been about enough. But this vicious man, they saw him, too — at least, Danny Potter did. He didn't know who he was. You see, he was using a rifle," he said slowly. "He stood up to aim, and his hat fell off. He'd a bald head, Danny says. The fog was gone and there was a glimmer of moon, and he'd a bald head."

"A rifle?" Mat echoed. Dick Ackley was staring at the inspector, imagining what had happened.

"He wasn't aiming at the boys, not exactly. The boat. They were away out. It was three o'clock in the morning. They were in deep water. All he cared about was hitting the boat, and that he did. He put five big holes in her. One bullet hit young Sissle's arm, but it was the boat the man was after."

Meg had been sitting as if she were frozen. Now she said, "But to put holes in their boat — with a rifle — away out at sea —"

"Yes, girl. Indeed, so. She started to fill with water very quick. He waited around a few minutes, but she settled fast.

Then he swung round his launch and gunned the motor and was off, and there they were, the boys from Charity's, without a hope in the world."

"But they . . . they're still . . ." Meg said.

"They had their oars, girl. Four strong oars to cling to. The water is perishing cold in our sea. They couldn't have lasted long. But the sea in summer is not as lonely as it looks. When they were about done, a trawler making for Argentia, away around the coast, came by and spotted them. No radio on the craft, a slow craft, too. So it's taken a while to make port and get word to us. There's a road to Argentia; I've sent a car for the lads. They'll do fine. And, when we pick up this gentleman, even if some way he manages to diddle us about other things, we've got witnesses." He laughed. "And strong witnesses. It takes a long time to get a good new boat and all the fishing gear in a little Outport like Charity's. Those boys worked in the Maine woods a good many winters to save money to buy that boat. They'll not forget that she's gone, nor who is responsible."

Tim's throat had loosened. It was going to work all right, without choking him up with tears, like a baby. He said, "Out of all that great big treasure, sir, could Mr. Jones bear to give away enough to buy a new red boat?"

The inspector's eyes suddenly didn't say anything. He had to decide what could be told and what couldn't. Finally, "When it's decided who owns that treasure, there'll be plenty set aside for proper rewards, boy. Had you thought of that?"

Dick Ackley laughed. "I'd be willing to bet a plugged nickel, Inspector, that that's the last thing these three *have* thought of."

CHAPTER
15

THE SMALL PLANE touched down lightly at the Cornerbrook Airport. There were six people aboard; Inspector Fitzgerald, Mr. Lewis Jones, Dick Ackley and the three children. This was highly irregular, the inspector had said; the children had no place here. But as Dick Ackley had pointed out, he had no place here either, except that after being suspected and accused of crime, he was going to insist on being in at the finish. As for the children, it was all their story. They had a right to see the end.

There were two police cars waiting, filled with big solid-looking men, all armed, Tim was sure. The children couldn't be allowed to ride in a police car. They got into another car with Dick Ackley, a car one of the police borrowed for him. The little procession set out for the highway; for the road from St. John's. It was 565 miles from St. John's to Port aux

Basques; Cornerbrook was on the way. A car leaving St. John's on Sunday morning, fairly early, could get to Cornerbrook about now. The Manren car was, actually, approaching; the highway police had spotted it and had kept reporting on it for the past hour. It was only two miles away.

The police cars went forward. Dick Ackley, instructed to keep well in the rear, was excited. He said, "You kids have had what might be called a rewarding time. If I may make so bold, may I have the exclusive rights to your story? I'll give you half my royalties, or all of them, if you insist. You've dug up one of the stories of the century. You've very likely found the Lost Loot of Lima! Frozen Face Jones won't tell me and the inspector obviously has been told to keep his mouth shut, but I'm sure you found the Loot of Lima."

"We don't know what we're allowed to tell," Meg said politely.

"We'll have to talk it all over with Dad," Tim said.

"You don't really need us," Mat said. "The Tourist Bureau will probably turn the cave into a special place, maybe with a tollgate at the front door and the back door."

"A nice progressive idea," Dick Ackley said, and grinned. He took a long breath.

Coming toward them, barely in sight, the big station wagon was moving along the road. It wasn't shiny now. There was a lot of dust on the road between here and St. John's. There hadn't been any danger, after all, Inspector Fitzgerald had said, that the car could be anywhere but here; there weren't any side roads, or at least none that led to any place where there would be a big boat to take the

151

station wagon off the island. There was only the ferry at Port aux Basques.

Dick Ackley said carefully, "A man is not of the highest intelligence when he leaves himself only one bolt hole. Now, if I'd found that cave, I had the perfect setup. My pal, Tommy Malone, coming in to St. John's for me with his yacht — quite a big yacht, too, and having to take on stores — well, I could have slid out from under like an eel . . ." he stopped. He turned and stared down at Tim, sitting beside him. Tim grinned.

From the back seat Mat said, "That was the idea."

"You weren't missing much, were you? You gave me a bad few hours, you young rogues."

The station wagon had been sailing right along. Now the two black police cars were approaching it. They divided, one to the right, one to the left. They stopped in an angle, blocking the road.

The station wagon stopped.

The doors opened. Mr. Manren, tall, paunchy, but still elegant, stepped out on one side. The inspector and the policemen were all standing in the road. Mrs. Manren got out her door and stood looking at them.

There wasn't going to be any trouble. Mr. Manren looked terrified, white, like a cornered animal. He didn't produce a gun. He didn't do anything, just stood there.

Dick Ackley drove closer. He got out of the car. The children followed him. They walked down the road. The Manrens were staring at them.

The inspector was saying something to them, something the children couldn't hear. He was just questioning them, wasn't he?

152

It was Mrs. Manren who saw the children first. She turned whitish-yellow, like old buttermilk, stale and sour. Then, not knowing what she was doing, she screamed. It was a terrible scream. She said, "You fool! You fool, Randle, they're still alive!"

After a second Dick Ackley said soberly, "That does it, I should think."

But Mr. Lewis Jones wasn't satisfied yet. He had the men look over the station wagon right then and there. It had false floorboards. And under them was a telltale layer of gold bars and a dozen flat parcels of coins and jewels.

The whole story was told.

It unreeled itself like a movie in Tim's mind. It was all clear. There was only one thing he had to say.

He said it. "Dick That man give me a ten-dollar bill. He said it was to buy flowers for my mother. That's what he said." His throat began to hurt. He looked at Dick Ackley carefully.

"Yes," Dick said. "Yes, he would do that. A ten-dollar bill. To buy flowers for your mother." He laughed, a short angry laugh. "I don't think it was quite enough," he said.

CHAPTER

16

Big Ben Patterson, tanned so dark he looked like an Indian chief, came back from Labrador ten days after all the excitement was over. He sat in the living room of their hotel suite on his first evening and listened to the whole long story. Everybody told it to him, talking at once. It took a while for the story to come clear. Ben Patterson's face changed from grim to gay a dozen times as he listened.

He said at last, "I'd heard of the Loot of Lima. It's an old story. You say they still don't know for sure if that's what you found?"

"Maybe what we found was kind of a mixed-up loot," Tim said. "That's all Inspector Fitzgerald would say. It's going to take an awful long time to get it all identified and sent where it belongs." He looked at Meg and Mat, sitting on the edge of their chairs. "By the way, Dad, this Inspector Fitzgerald is a kind of relation of ours."

155

"Oh?" Big Ben Patterson said. He glanced at his wife. "Some more Newfoundland cousins, Lucy?"

She laughed. "Not exactly. The children have been listening to some very ancient history."

"It's just that we're all Carews," Tim explained.

"And we've got royalty in us," Mat said.

"You see, Mom is the descendant of a very, very beautiful princess," Meg told him.

"Well, that's not hard to believe," he said. He frowned. "Where did you get this ancient history?"

"From Dick Ackley. His name is really Richard Hakluyt, you know, like the man who wrote the *Voyages*," Mat explained. "It was changed from Hakluyt to Ackley. Lots of names get changed."

"I see. And who is this beautiful princess? Anybody I might know about?"

"She was Welsh. Her father was a Welsh king. Her name was Nest."

Big Ben Patterson grinned. "Seems to me I've heard about her. She was quite a girl. Was she a Carew?"

"Well, not exactly. She was just Nest. But she married a man named Gerald, and some of her children were called *Fitz*gerald — that means son of Gerald — " Mat said, "and one of them was called Carew after a castle he owned. And the Carews were ancestors of the Raleighs and the Drakes and the Grenvilles . . ." He took a long breath. "I think history's going to be a lot more fun, next year. I think it is."

"What about Sir Wilfred Grenfell? The famous medical missionary to Labrador? Was he a Grenville?"

Tim sat thinking. He looked at Mat. Names got changed. They certainly did.

"Of course," his father said, "Sir Wilfred Grenfell was

156

only born about a hundred years ago. You're talking about people away back."

"When I get home, I'm going to find out," Tim said. "I bet he was a Grenville. Dad, why did that special family of people care so much about Newfoundland? Why?"

"It's no use asking me. I'm a geologist, not a genealogist. But there would have been a fine reason."

"A lot of their relatives came and settled Newfoundland. Mr. Ackley can tell by the names here now. Crocker and Kellaway and Crewe —"

Meg said dreamily, "I'm going to find out everything about the Princess Nest. I think it's exciting, having a princess for an ancestor, a real live princess."

Her father put his arm around her shoulders and gave her a quick hug. His eyes twinkled. "It's exciting," he said. "But it's not very special, is it? Everybody in Newfoundland likely has that princess for an ancestor, or some other one. Maybe everybody, if you go back far enough, has at least one princess for an ancestor. So don't put your chin too high, Meggie." He got up. "I'm hungry," he said. "I've been living on bacon and beans for three weeks. Let's all go down and have dinner."

Mat said in a small voice, "It's Friday, Dad. It's the day they serve The Fish."

"Well," his father said, "what's the matter with The Fish? There's not a better meal to be had in the world than the Fish of Newfoundland."

DATE DUE

JAN 2 9 1966			
FEB 1 5 1966			C
FEB 2 8 1966			
MAR 2 1 1966			T
JUN 6 1966			
AUG 2 9 1966			
NOV 3 1966			
JUL 1 0 1967			
NOV 2 0 1967			
MAY 1 6 1968			
JUN 2 4 1968			
AUG 1 3 1970			
SE 28 '82			
AP 14 '84			
AG 20 '84			
MR 02 '85			
AG 06 '86			
AG 23 '86			
GAYLORD			PRINTED IN U.S.A.